GHOST TOWNS
of the
MOUNTAIN WEST

Your Guide to the Hidden History
and Old West Haunts of Colorado, Wyoming,
Idaho, Montana, Utah, and Nevada

Text and Photography
by Philip Varney

Voyageur Press

First published in 2010 by Voyageur Press, an imprint of MBI Publishing Company, 400 First Avenue North, Suite 300, Minneapolis, MN 55401 USA

Voyageur Press titles are also available at discounts in bulk quantity for industrial or sales-promotional use. For details write to Special Sales Manager at MBI Publishing Company, 400 First Avenue North, Suite 300, Minneapolis, MN 55401 USA.

To find out more about our books, visit us online at www.voyageurpress.com.

ISBN 978-0-7603-3358-7

    Library of Congress Cataloging-in-Publication Data

Varney, Philip.
 Ghost towns of the mountain West : your guide to the hidden history and Old West haunts of Colorado, Wyoming, Idaho, Montana, Utah, and Nevada /
Philip Varney.
    p. cm.
 Includes bibliographical references and index.
 ISBN 978-0-7603-3358-7 (softback : alk. paper)
 1. Ghost towns—West (U.S.)—Guidebooks. 2. West (U.S.)—Guidebooks. 3. West (U.S.)—History, Local. I. Title.
 F590.7.V37 2010
 978—dc27
            2009018622

Edited by Danielle Ibister
Designed by Pauline Molinari
Design Manager: LeAnn Kuhlmann
Cartographer: Patti Isaacs, Parrot Graphics

Front cover main: The Elkhorn Barber Shop, Sullivan's Saddlery, and the jail in Nevada City, Montana.
Front cover bottom left: The one-room schoolhouse in Nevada City, Montana.
Front cover bottom right: A gravestone in Utah's Frisco Cemetery.
Back cover top: The Carissa Saloon, South Pass City, Wyoming.
Back cover bottom left: The Commodore Mine Operation on the Bachelor Historic Loop, Colorado.
Back cover bottom right: Silverton's Hillside Cemetery, Colorado.
Page 1: The once-bustling business district of Nevada's Belmont.
Page 2: Idaho's Bayhorse Hotel.
Page 3: The parlor of Silver City's Idaho Hotel. The poker table dates from 1878 and has a lock box underneath the tabletop.
Opposite: Brothers Roy and Tony Stark, along with their sister, Annabelle, kept this store open into the 1950s as the last business in St. Elmo, Colorado.

Printed in China

FOR MY SISTER, MARY LEVINE.

CONTENTS

TO THE READER

In the summer of 1955, I sat in the back seat of a brand-new Buick as I accompanied my best friend on his family's vacation. I was eleven at the time, and this young Illinois boy had never seen a mountain. I watched in disbelief as the plains of eastern Colorado began to display an astonishing western horizon.

We stayed for a week at a dude ranch somewhere near Idaho Springs. We took a Jeep trip to an old mine. We visited Central City, with its crumbling, empty buildings—only a few open for the occasional curious tourist. I had seen my first ghost town.

I have never been quite the same since. My family moved three years later to Arizona, and I couldn't wait to see places like the ghost town of Jerome. Twenty-one years after that, I found myself teaching high school English in Tucson and writing a book about Arizona ghost towns. Its opening entry: Jerome.

I wrote that first ghost town book, *Arizona's Best Ghost Towns,* in response to my frustration with the way other such books are generally organized: Most of them had the ghost towns listed alphabetically, not organized geographically, which seemed far more logical to me. Some books had their maps buried in the back, instead of up with the ghost towns themselves. I wanted a completely practical, informative guide that would give me everything I needed next to me on the seat of my truck. That first book's success led to six more.

My previous books did not attempt the scope that this book does. Four covered one state only (Arizona [twice], New Mexico, and Colorado); two books were necessary for one state (Southern and Northern California); and my most recent book covered two states and part of a province (Washington, Oregon, and southern British Columbia).

The book you have in your hands is similar to those earlier books in that it arranges towns geographically, so you can visit places in logical groups. Each chapter features a map of the area, a history of each town, a description of what remains at the site when I visited, and specific directions to each site. But it is vastly different from my other books because it, of necessity, has to be exclusive. It could not possibly contain all of the ghost town sites in all six states it covers. If you want to find more sites than I have featured here, there are many books that cover one state only. All the books I recommend are listed in the bibliography at the end of this book.

A very restorable Chevrolet pickup rests in the weeds in one of Nevada's best ghost towns, Belmont.

You might be interested to know, for this book, how I selected which towns to include and which to exclude. To begin, if there is very little left at a site, it's not going to be included unless it is in proximity to another, better site. For example, Bonanza, Idaho, doesn't offer much in the way of ruins, but it's adjacent to an outstanding dredge and it's just down the road from Custer, a rewarding town to explore, so I include it in chapter 5.

At the other end of the spectrum are former ghost town sites that have been thrust into the twenty-first century, having rebounded into modernity. Aspen, Breckenridge, Crested Butte, and Telluride all were once nearly abandoned, as hard as that may be to believe, and all were included in my book *Ghost Towns of Colorado* but are not in this volume. I did, however, include several communities that have that elusive "ghost town feeling," places that retain considerable charm despite their modern touches. Examples are Colorado's Leadville, Lake City, and Silverton; Idaho's Idaho City; Utah's Spring City; and Montana's and Nevada's towns both named Virginia City.

I also omitted many towns that I have enjoyed visiting but where I felt the buildings weren't sufficiently distinct architecturally. These were the most difficult towns to exclude, because virtually all ghost towns are interesting at some level. So, to fans of Colorado's Ashcroft and Independence, Idaho's Warren, and Nevada's Manhattan, all I can say is that I had to eliminate towns, and these were some of the last to go. I was standing in each of them when I made my decision.

A person new to ghost town hunting might tour the first entry in this book, Central City, and wonder just what I consider a ghost town to be, because Central City has shops, restaurants, and numerous casinos. By my definition, a ghost town has two characteristics: The population has decreased markedly, and the initial reason for its settlement (such as mining) no longer keeps people there. At the peak of its mining frenzy, Central City had an estimated population of 30,000 citizens; now 515 people live there, and virtually no one makes a living in a mine. A ghost town, then, can be completely deserted, like Carson, Colorado; it can have a few residents, like Silver City, Idaho; it can be protected for posterity by a state government, like Bannack, Montana; or it can have genuine signs of vitality, like Austin, Nevada. But in each case, the town is a shadow of its former self. These four examples were all mining towns, and their boom has long since passed.

The residents living in sleepy places like Colorado's Silver Plume, Idaho's Clayton, Utah's Spring City, or Nevada's Goldfield may be offended about inclusion in a "ghost town" book. But their communities have "ghost town" indicators: In each case, the population has dropped precipitously, and once-prosperous businesses have closed. In each of the four towns, their historic school has no students.

Miners working at Summitville—elevation 11,300 feet—had only these modest shacks to brave Colorado's winter storms.

Some guidebooks I have used when traveling in the West were apparently written principally for armchair travelers. Unfortunately, some have been written by armchair authors. I cringe when I realize that a book I'm using has been written by someone who obviously hasn't personally observed what he is writing about. I first saw some of the sites in this book in the late 1970s. But I visited or revisited every single site in 2007 and 2008. The color photographs in this book, unless noted in the photo's caption, were all taken within that same time period. The book's emphasis is on what remains at a town, not what was there in its heyday. I describe what to look for at each site, and in most towns I suggest walking and driving tours.

TO THE READER

Patent medicines on display in a Georgetown, Colorado, store promise relief from a host of maladies.

I also make recommendations about museums, train rides, and mine or mill tours. To see them all would be expensive and somewhat repetitious, so when such attractions come up, I give advice based on comparisons to similar tours. My observations are candid, and I received no special consideration at such sites. I paid for all attractions, and guides knew me only as another tourist.

Almost every town has a cemetery. Some of my most poignant moments have come while walking around graveyards, since emotions are often laid bare on tombstones. To read the grief of parents in the epitaphs of their children is to see the West in absolutely personal terms. History comes tragically alive in cemeteries.

Here's a time breakdown: To visit all of the sites in this book without frantically racing from one to another, I would estimate that you would need about twelve days in Colorado, three days in Wyoming, six days in Idaho, five days in Montana, four days in Utah, and six days in Nevada. I took months longer and drove thousands of miles farther than you need to, but then I was looking at many ghost towns that I eliminated (170 in all). I also needed to photograph in optimum light, so seeing a wonderful, photogenic place like Comet, Montana, at high noon was not acceptable.

Why are we called to these places where so many lives have toiled and so many have been forgotten? My late friend, mystery writer Tony Hillerman, in a foreword to my book *New Mexico's Best Ghost Towns*, captured the answer:

> To me, to many of my friends, to scores of thousands of Americans, these ghost towns offer a sort of touching-place with the past. We stand in their dust and try to project our imagination backward into what they were long ago. Now and then, if the mood and the light and the weather are exactly right, we almost succeed.

Our "touching-places with the past," however, are in immediate and long-term danger. Vandals tear up floorboards hoping for a nonexistent coin. Looters remove an old door with the vague notion of using it, only to discard it later. Thieves dislodge a child's headstone, heartlessly assuming no one will miss it.

Remember, these old towns are to be explored and photographed but also protected and treasured. You must be a part of the preservation, not the destruction. As you visit the places in this book, please remember that ghost towns are extremely fragile. Leave a site as you found it. I have seen many items on the backroads that tempted me, but I have no collection of artifacts. If you must pick up something, how about a film wrapper or an aluminum can?

When I was doing fieldwork for my book *Ghost Towns of Colorado,* I found the following notice posted in a lovely but deteriorating house. It eloquently conveys what our deportment should be at ghost towns and other historic spots:

> Attention: We hope that you are enjoying looking at our heritage. The structure may last many more years for others to see and enjoy if everyone like you treads lightly and takes only memories and pictures.

—Philip Varney
Tucson

A word to my readers who own Ghost Towns of Colorado, *published in 1999: That book features almost a hundred ghost towns. This book showcases sixteen Colorado sites. Although there are changes to the text for each site, especially concerning updates on walking and driving tours, the historical information is virtually the same. You will be reading lots of repeat information. But each site was revisited in 2008, and all of the photographs are new.*

INTRODUCTION

THE ROCKY MOUNTAINS AND THE GREAT BASIN

Not long after the Louisiana Purchase was completed in 1803, President Thomas Jefferson sent the Corps of Discovery, led by Captains Meriwether Lewis and William Clark, to explore the northwest portion of the purchase and to find a route to the Pacific Ocean. The area west of the purchase (then called Oregon Country, which was essentially today's Oregon, Washington, and British Columbia) was, at that time, claimed by both the United States and England.

The Corps of Discovery's route included crossing what would become Montana, Idaho, and Wyoming. (Incidentally, Sacagawea, the Shoshone woman who was instrumental in that expedition's success, was born near what is now Salmon, Idaho.) The Corps of Discovery firmly established the United States' land claims in 1805 and also kindled the interest of fur traders. Trappers and explorers, popularly known as mountain men, began to explore the Rocky Mountains in about 1810 and led the way to establishing trade routes and constructing trading posts. Some were independent, but most were employed by fur companies. Legends were told about mountain men Jim Bridger, Jedediah Smith, and John Johnson, the latter made famous in the fictionalized film account of his life, *Jeremiah Johnson*.

The Great Basin, most of which lies in Nevada and the western portion of Utah, was considered by the early explorers who saw it as worthless, essentially uninhabitable, and best left to the nomadic Native Americans who roamed it. Smith crossed it, as did military expeditions, one led by Captain John Frémont and his guide, Kit Carson. Frémont's expeditions explored and mapped much of the Great Basin, and it was he who determined that the basin had no outlet to any sea.

In 1841, Congress passed the Pre-emption Act, which permitted white males, widows, and female heads of families to claim 160 acres of public land for farming purposes. Two years later a westward movement, known as the Great Migration, began, commencing from Independence, Missouri, along the Oregon Trail to Oregon. Frémont and Carson led one of the early expeditions. For three decades, more than three hundred thousand settlers took the two-thousand-mile journey with the promise of a new Eden.

One of the loveliest gravestones in the Mountain West is in Nevada's Austin Cemetery. This angel stands over Mrs. L. W. Compton, a native of County Limerick, Ireland, who died in 1900 at the age of fifty-six.

What might have seemed an insignificant moment in New York in 1830 proved to have an enormous effect in Utah in 1847: Joseph Smith, in Palmyra, New York, founded what would become the Church of Jesus Christ of Latter-day Saints. Although he was killed in Carthage, Illinois, his practitioners followed his successor, Brigham Young, to the Salt Lake Valley and found Utah, the only state among the six featured in this book settled primarily by families. The early arrivals in the other Mountain West states tended to be young, single, and male. One pioneer lad inscribed in his diary, "Got nearer to a female this evening than I have been for six months. Came near fainting."

In 1849, gold was discovered in Coloma, California, attracting more hopeful emigrants along the Oregon Trail. The movement became the greatest migration of people in the history of the Western Hemisphere.

For argonauts heading to California, the Rocky Mountains were an obstacle to avoid or overcome. After those mountains came the Great Basin, which was either crossed at one's peril or avoided by staying north of it.

As famous as the Gold Rush of 1849 is, it was rather brief for most of those who trouped there. As a result, disappointed prospectors began to look north and east from California for the new El Dorado.

Although there were small strikes in Oregon (1851) and British Columbia (1858), the larger jackpots were found in what would become the states of the Mountain West. Colorado was first, in the spring of 1859, followed just a few months later with Nevada's astonishing Comstock Lode.

The "Pikes Peak or Bust" frenzy was fueled by an estimated one hundred thousand people, mostly young men, who crossed the Kansas Territory's dusty plains to the foot of the Rockies in 1859. About three-quarters ultimately went home disappointed because of exaggerated accounts. (Mark Twain defined a mine as "a hole in the ground owned by a liar.") There were, however, success stories, and they fill Colorado's history books.

Nevada's rush came originally from prospectors and then miners (for there is a difference) from the nearly tapped-out Mother Lode in California. The silver that was found in the Comstock Lode played a significant role in bankrolling the Union in the Civil War.

Idaho City, Idaho, and Bannack, Montana, each had gold strikes in 1862, bringing hopeful hordes to those respective areas. In both cases, prospectors then fanned out from those bonanzas to find more gold and silver in surrounding hills.

Utah's mining began with soldiers from the California and Nevada Volunteers, who, with the blessing of their leader, Colonel Patrick E. O'Connor, filed claims southwest of the

Great Salt Lake in 1863. Originally, Brigham Young had instructed his followers not to seek the riches of precious metal mining, so many of the original strikes in the Utah Territory were made by non-Mormons. After Young's death in 1877, Mormon Church members and even church leaders became involved in silver mines. In the twentieth century, copper became Utah's bonanza.

Gold seekers who had used the Oregon Trail passed right over a major gold deposit in Wyoming that wasn't discovered until 1868 near South Pass. That discovery led to others in Wyoming, although coal turned out to be the state's major mining product.

Inventions in the industrialized world had an enormous effect upon the United States, nowhere more dramatically than in the American West. Vastly improved communication came with Samuel Morse's improved electromagnetic telegraph in 1832 and Alexander Graham Bell's patenting of the telephone in 1876. Mining gained a powerful force for moving earth with the invention of dynamite in 1867 by Swedish chemist Alfred Nobel.

But nothing changed the American West as much as the completion of the first Transcontinental Railroad in 1869. The British publication *The Economist*, in the middle of the nineteenth century, commented that in the 1820s the speed a man could go unaided was about four miles per hour, "the same as Adam." By horse, it was up to about ten miles per hour for any significant distance. But, *The Economist* went on, by the 1850s, a man could, by train, habitually go forty miles per hour and occasionally as high as *seventy*.

The Transcontinental Railroad linked the Midwest to California. The journey that argonauts had made in 1849 to the Gold Rush, which took an average of about a hundred days, was reduced to seven days. Stagecoach lines became obsolete. The Oregon Trail became a relic. And the effect upon mining was enormous: With railroads to carry supplies in and ore out, costs were significantly decreased. Ore that had previously been too expensive to mine, mill, and smelt could now yield a healthy profit.

Nevertheless, mining towns are created to fail, as they exist to extract a finite quantity, and when that quantity is gone, the town is doomed—unless it can find another way to prosper.

To experience the Mountain West's history, one can explore its remnants: the mining camps, railroad ghosts, and farming towns that were all but abandoned in search of more promising places. The tent camps have disappeared. The majority of the wood-frame towns have vanished as well, having fallen to fire, vandalism, or salvage. Some delightful towns still exist, however, and the best are showcased in this book.

1

COLORADO

G H O S T S O F

THE FIRST
BONANZAS

GOLD FEVER! THIS IS WHERE THE COLORADO GOLD RUSH BEGAN, the "Pikes Peak or Bust" frenzy that brought a hundred thousand people to Colorado in 1859 alone. In January of that year, placer gold discoveries along Clear Creek gave rise to Idaho Springs, a delightful former mining town now located right along Interstate 70. Five months after the Clear Creek discovery, lode gold was found where Central City now stands. (Note: For the definition of mining terms like "placer" and "lode," consult the glossary terms on pages 309–311.)

As prospectors poured into the area, late arrivals expanded the boundaries of the excitement, searching for the next big strike. Not long after the Central City bonanza, Clear Creek gold seekers found pay dirt upriver from Idaho Springs, and Georgetown and its sister community of Silver Plume were born.

Fairplay and Leadville were also founded in the early boom times, but their real prosperity came later, with gold dredging in Fairplay in the 1870s and with enormous silver strikes in Leadville in 1877. All of the sites in this chapter offer excellent historic buildings and a genuine "touching-place" with Colorado's past, none more so than Fairplay's South Park City, one of the finest pioneer museums in the American West.

Baby Doe Tabor was told by her dying husband, Horace, to hold on to Leadville's Matchless Mine at all costs. She became a pauper, freezing to death in the building at the left rear, still heeding her husband's advice.

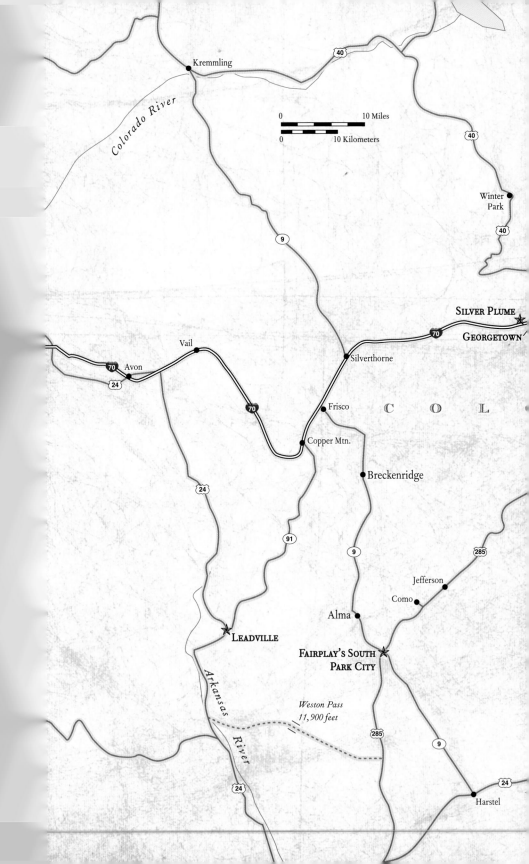

Kremmling

Colorado River

0   10 Miles
0   10 Kilometers

40

40

Winter
Park

40

9

SILVER PLUME

70   GEORGETOWN

Vail   Silverthorne

70   Avon   C   O   L

24   Frisco

70

Copper Mtn.

Breckenridge

24

91   285

9   Jefferson

Como

Alma

LEADVILLE

FAIRPLAY'S SOUTH
PARK CITY

285

Arkansas   9

Weston Pass
11,900 feet
285

River

24   Harstel

24

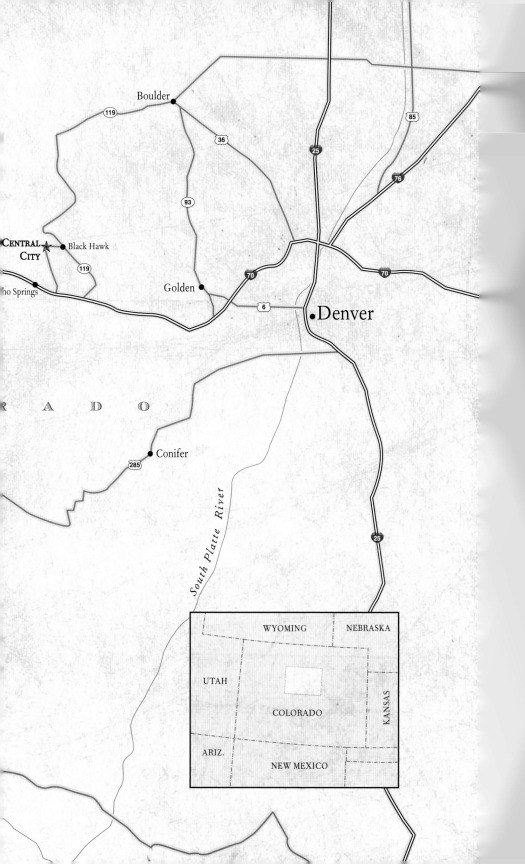

CENTRAL CITY

Central City and its next-door neighbor, Black Hawk, have been rivals since 1859. Their history and geography are so interconnected that it is impossible to write about one without including the other.

The rivalry has intensified in the last few years. When limited-stakes gambling came to the two towns in 1991, Black Hawk received a disproportionate amount of the revenue, partially because Denverites arrived at Black Hawk first. Central City responded with an enormously expensive parkway designed to ignore Black Hawk's existence (no mention of the town is made on any of the billboards along the way) and bring gamblers into Central City first. Has the gamble paid off? I followed about ten autos on the parkway, and not one stopped in Central City; they all continued down the road to its rival. That is hardly a scientific study. But for every dollar gambled in Central City in 2008, seven dollars were spent in Black Hawk. At this writing, many buildings in Central City are vacant. Perhaps it will return to the near-ghost town status it experienced in the mid-twentieth century.

Black Hawk, for those interested in historic buildings, has paid a steep price for its gambling success. It still has some good buildings of antiquity, but they are harder and harder to find. Central City has kept its soul, but Black Hawk has not. A Denver cartoonist captured the feeling with a drawing of a string of glitzy casinos with the caption, "Did they have to kill Black Hawk to save it?"

In January 1859, placer gold discoveries were made along Clear Creek near what is now Idaho Springs, and on May 6 of that year, Georgian John H. Gregory staked a claim that established the first gold lode in Colorado. The excitement along Clear Creek turned into a mad rush in Gregory Gulch. Several thousand prospectors were at work in less than a month. Within two months, thirty thousand people were fueling the gold frenzy in what was called the Richest Square Mile on Earth.

The camp that formed was Gregory Diggings, later called Mountain City. A Gregory Diggings post office was established in January 1860, but the town was simply absorbed by Central City, its neighbor to the west. Central City was likely named because it was central among area mining camps. Black Hawk was a secondary part of the gold rush. Located down the gulch from Gregory Diggings, it was probably named because a mill erected there came from the Black Hawk

Company of Rock Island, Illinois. While water was scarce to its upper-gulch neighbors, Black Hawk had an abundant supply, as it was located along the North Branch of Clear Creek. Because it had the enormous quantities of water necessary to power several mills, Black Hawk became known as the City of Mills.

When early surface gold and easily retrieved primary deposits along Gregory Gulch were depleted, miners found that the remaining hard-rock veins contained complex sulfide ores. The initial mining boom was over.

In 1867, however, Nathaniel Hill, a Brown University professor, put his theories of extracting gold from sulfide ore into practice by erecting in Black Hawk the first successful smelter in the territory, the Boston and Colorado Smelting Works. This solidified Black Hawk's importance in a rebounding mining industry. Ore could now be shipped in concentrate, significantly lowering transportation costs.

The result was another boost in the economies of both cities. Black Hawk was relegated, however, to blue-collar status, while Central City became the grand lady of the Rockies, with a luxury hotel and an opulent opera house. While Black Hawk could claim Colorado's first permanent school, Central City residents could sneer that although theirs was second, it was made of stone, not merely a wood frame.

The best ore bodies near Central City were depleted by the 1880s; from then until the early 1900s, area mines were steady producers, but the bonanza times were over. Mining continued as shafts went deeper, but inflation and the unchanging price of gold made mining less profitable. Before and after World War I, buildings in both towns were dismantled and moved to other communities. Although mining continued on a lesser scale, Central City and Black Hawk seemed headed toward obscurity.

Tourism brought the area somewhat back to life beginning in the 1950s, when I first gaped at the towns as a wide-eyed eleven-year-old. They were then dying, but not dead, as curious visitors glimpsed a past that was colorful but, for the townspeople, not particularly profitable.

When casino gambling came to Central City and Black Hawk, the stakes literally changed, for better or worse. Today the Richest Square Mile on Earth doesn't try to remove pockets of gold from the hills; it tries to remove the gold from your pockets. Central City is the star for the ghost town enthusiast, where you can find, well, a jackpot of history.

Casinos occupy several of the historic buildings, many dating from 1874, of Central City's Main Street. This photo was taken before the casinos opened and the shuttle buses arrived, bringing hopeful gamblers.

WALKING AND DRIVING AROUND CENTRAL CITY

A good place to begin your tour of Central City is the Schoolhouse Museum (open daily during the summer), which is located on High Street, one block north of the highway, where you will find displays and memorabilia provided by the Gilpin County Historical Society. Downtown Central City features many buildings from the gold rush days. Two structures of particular interest are the Teller House and the Central City Opera House, both located on Eureka Street. Summer tours of the buildings begin on the hour at the Teller House. The Teller House, built in 1872, was considered one of the West's finest hotels. When President Ulysses S. Grant visited in 1873, silver bricks worth sixteen thousand dollars were placed so he would have a path appropriate for a president as he walked from his carriage to the Teller House. Because gold made Central City famous, he is supposed to have inquired why they had chosen silver. The answer? Gold was too common.

The 750-seat opera house was constructed in 1878 by Cornish stonemasons and features a central chandelier, hickory chairs, and decorative murals. Known for its excellent acoustics, it is still in use.

Beyond the opera house at 209 Eureka Street is the 1874 Thomas-Billings House, which was a wedding present in the early 1890s to Marcia Billings and her husband, Ben Thomas, from her parents. The furnishings are virtually complete, with more than four thousand items belonging to the Thomases. (The home is open for tours on weekends in the summer.)

This marker was erected in the City of Central Cemetery for siblings who died in 1872 and 1875, respectively. Their stone reads: "Sleep on, sweet babes and take thy rest / For such as thee the Savior blessed."

Eureka Street continues northwest for a mile from Central City to six of its seven cemeteries. The cemeteries fan out around a triangle intersection of roads. Starting across from the Boodle Mill, the graveyard farthest to the northwest is the International Order of Odd Fellows (IOOF) cemetery. One headstone there consists of an unusual log cabin for William R. Walter, who died in 1899 at twenty-one years of age. Another marker is for Sarah Stevens. She was born in 1796, the earliest birth date I can recall on a Colorado headstone. She died in 1872.

East of the IOOF graveyard is a small cemetery for the Red Man Lodge. Behind it is the large Catholic cemetery, where many natives of Italy, Ireland, and Germany are buried. The most interesting feature here is a double-thick brick beehive ovenlike structure. According to local author-historian Alan Granruth, its purpose is a mystery. He thinks perhaps it served as a temporary burial location during winter months when digging a grave in the frozen ground would have been difficult. It is also conceivable that it simply predates the cemetery and was a kiln used to convert wood to charcoal. (For more on that process, see the Piedmont, Wyoming, entry, pages 136–139.)

The Knights of Pythias cemetery is across the road to the east. Adjacent to it is the City of Central Cemetery. Most of the older graves are found in the southeast corner. Beyond that cemetery is a small graveyard for the Ancient Order of the Foresters.

Central City's Masonic cemetery is on the other side of town. At the beginning of the Central City Parkway is a turnoff to the small ghost town of Nevadaville. Just before you reach a curious stone structure on your left (which may have been a Buddhist temple), you will see a road to your right, which leads to the cemetery. There I found something quite touching that I have not seen before: Thomas and Elizabeth Warren buried their daughter Minnie in 1876 after fourteen months of life. They named their next daughter Minnie as well, and she died in 1877 at only eight months of age.

WHEN YOU GO

From Denver, take Interstate 70 west for about 30 miles to Exit 243 and follow the Central City Parkway for 8.1 miles to Central City.

GEORGETOWN

Georgetown displays Colorado's best china and finest crystal. Hardly a mere "mining camp," it has an elegance and a refinement that few other towns can match. Up the hill from Georgetown is Silver Plume, whose architecture may lack the finesse of its sister to the east, but its main street looks like what people expect from the frontier American West.

Brothers George and David Griffith, farmers from Bourbon County, Kentucky, headed to the newly discovered gold fields of Colorado in 1859 only to find that the best claims around Central City and Idaho Springs were already taken. So they prospected farther west up Clear Creek where, in June of the same year, they found placer gold. They staked a claim and established the Griffith

The Fish Block, built in 1889 by banker Charles Fish, stands at the corner of Sixth and Rose streets. Behind it stands the 1891 Masonic Hall.

Mining District. Their gold discovery, however, was to be the only important one in the district.

As others joined them, a camp grew, known as George's Town (named after the older brother). A second community, called Elizabethtown (probably named for the Griffiths' sister), came to life south of the first camp when silver was discovered there in 1864. These were the first mines in Colorado in which silver was mined as the principal ore, not as a lesser byproduct to gold.

In 1868, Georgetown and Elizabethtown consolidated as one community. That same year, Georgetown displaced Idaho Springs as the seat of Clear Creek County in a bitter election. By 1870, the population had climbed to eight hundred, and Georgetown settled in as "Queen of the Silver Camps." (Leadville, featured on pages 48–55, was to become the "King.") In that year, Georgetown citizens presented a silver spike to commemorate the rail link between Denver and Cheyenne that joined Colorado to the Union Pacific Railroad and therefore to the rest of the nation.

By 1880, the population of Georgetown had soared to more than three thousand. The town had schools, churches, and hotels, as well as one saloon for every one hundred and fifty citizens. Four independent fire companies helped the community avoid a major conflagration.

In 1893, however, disaster of another variety hit Georgetown. A steady decline in silver prices, due to increased supply and decreased coinage, culminated in the repeal of the Sherman Silver Purchase Act. This act had guaranteed acquisition of almost nine million ounces of silver per month by the federal government. Its repeal meant that the coin of the realm was gold—and only gold. This was a major blow, not just to Georgetown but to the entire state; at the time, Colorado had been producing an astonishing 58 percent of the nation's silver. Mines and mills closed, and miners departed to gold fields in Cripple Creek and Victor (see chapter 2, pages 60–67). Georgetown went into a precipitous decline.

Not until the middle of the twentieth century did Georgetown bloom once again, this time as a mountain retreat and tourist attraction. It and Silver Plume were declared a National Historic Landmark District, and both civic groups and private individuals began in earnest to restore their lovely towns.

A delicate fountain and a solarium demonstrate the stately elegance of the Hamill House, an 1867 home that was extensively remodeled in 1878 and 1879 to become Georgetown's most elaborate residence. The stone building in the rear is the carriage house–stable.

The Gothic Revival–style six-hole outhouse at the Hamill House features a cantilevered overhang above its two entrances and a ventilating cupola.

The dining room of Georgetown's Hamill House. The 1879 original wallpaper had to be hand-painted after a 1974 fire caused smoke and water damage. The Renaissance Revival sideboard (left, rear) and the dining table are Hamill family originals.

WALKING AND DRIVING AROUND GEORGETOWN

As you enter Georgetown's historic district, turn left across Clear Creek and right on Rose Street, one of the two major residential avenues in Georgetown. (Taos Street, one block east, is the other.) Both streets have home after lovely home, whether modest or extravagant, featuring a wide variety of nineteenth-century architectural styles.

Rose Street leads to downtown, which you will want to tour by foot, not car. Start at the Community Center, formerly the 1868 courthouse, at Sixth and Argentine streets. There you can pick up brochures and a free walking tour map. (However, a more helpful tour guide on Georgetown and Silver Plume is for sale.) Historic photos are on display in the first-floor courtroom, where district court was held. The county courtroom, jury deliberation rooms, and public restrooms are upstairs.

Sixth Street contains too many fine commercial structures to enumerate here. If you go inside only one, visit the marvelous Hotel de Paris.

The grand hotel was brought into being by Frenchman Adolphe Francois Gerard, who immigrated to New York in 1868 at age twenty-two and headed west with the U.S. Cavalry. He deserted in Cheyenne, came to Denver in 1869, and changed his name to Louis Dupuy.

In 1873, Dupuy was working as a miner in Georgetown when he was injured in a dynamite explosion. He retired from mining and bought a small bakery, which over the years evolved into one of the finest hotels in the West. With Dupuy as owner and master chef, the Hotel de Paris served elegant dinners on Haviland china and featured gas lights, elaborately carved black walnut furniture, and hot and cold running water in each guest room—an almost unheard-of luxury.

Louis Dupuy died in 1900 at age fifty-six. He willed the hotel to his longtime housekeeper and friend Sophie Gally, who had also immigrated from France. She survived him by little more than five months. They are buried side by side in the Alvarado Cemetery north of town.

The Colonial Dames of America purchased the hotel in 1954 and began a thorough restoration. Touring the Hotel de Paris is a delight, from its guest rooms to wine cellar to kitchen to dining room to Dupuy's own quarters.

Across the street from the Hotel de Paris stands the 1866 Star Hook and Ladder Firehouse, now the town hall.

South of the main business district, on Fifth Street just west of Taos, is the 1874 Alpine Hose Company No. 2, which at this writing is being completely renovated. A sign announcing the remodel calls the building "the principal visual and historical symbol of Georgetown."

Some might argue that symbol is on Fourth Street, just east of Taos. The 1870 Maxwell House, a private residence closed to the public, is considered one of the country's ten best Victorian homes.

One residence open to the public and well worth touring is the opulent Hamill House, located at 305 Argentine Street, two blocks west of the Maxwell House.

A fairly modest home when it was constructed in 1867, the house became a showplace when it was remodeled and expanded in 1879 by its new owner, William A. Hamill, a prominent mine owner and silver speculator. The elegant Gothic mansion features a solarium, a schoolroom, and such refinements as central heating, a zinc-lined bathtub, and gold-plated doorknobs.

The Hamill House also has Colorado's most elaborate outhouse, a Gothic-styled six-seater with a cantilevered overhang above the entrance and a ventilating cupola. Later preservationists found pieces of expensive china, apparently broken by maids or scullions and dropped into the privy to conceal their clumsiness.

As mentioned earlier, Rose and Taos streets feature many exquisite private homes. Also on Taos are the 1869 wood-frame Grace Episcopal Church; the 1918 brick Catholic church; and the lovely, multisteepled, stone Presbyterian church , built between 1872 and 1874 (and the only Georgetown church in continuous service since its construction). Across the street from the Presbyterian church is the 1874 two-story Georgetown Public School (elementary grades on the first floor, high school on the second), which proudly asserts that it is a "State of Colorado Standard School Approved Class." At this writing, the school is being completely restored.

Also on Taos Street, across from the city park, is the Old Missouri Firehouse, built in 1875 to protect the north end of town.

If you wish to visit Georgetown's cemetery, drive toward the interstate onramp, but instead of going onto Interstate 70, proceed 3.2 miles north on Alvarado Road, which loosely parallels the highway.

The Alvarado Cemetery will be on your right with a conspicuous main gate. On the other side of the road is the old Georgetown Cemetery, which was relocated to this site in 1972 from the shore of Georgetown Lake.

The Alvarado Cemetery, like many large graveyards, is divided into sections for religious and fraternal groups. Hundreds of graves cover many acres, with considerable space between various sections. One of the first graves you will see, near a flagpole, is for David Griffith, the cofounder of Georgetown, who died in 1882.

In the Catholic section are the graves of Louis Dupuy, the celebrated owner of the Hotel de Paris, and his housekeeper, Sophie Gally. The headstone features two birds looking at each other and the inscription *Deux Bon Amis* (Two Good Friends).

To find Dupuy and Gally's graves, go about twenty yards from the main entrance and veer to the right about twelve yards toward a wrought-iron fence enclosing a grave. Beyond that, follow a road heading toward an aspen grove. About sixty-five yards from the wrought-iron fence, you will come to a large obelisk for William Spruance. Behind it and to the left is a bullet-shaped, terra cotta–colored marker about six and a half feet high for Dupuy and Gally.

WHEN YOU GO

Georgetown is 11.6 miles west of Idaho Springs and about 40 miles west of downtown Denver on Interstate 70.

The First United Presbyterian Church was dedicated upon its completion in 1874 after two years of construction. It was completely restored in 1974 to celebrate its centennial.

The Georgetown Loop Railroad and
Lebanon Silver Mine Tour

If you plan to ride only one tourist steam train in Colorado, consider this one. It is more affordable than the two deservedly famous trains in southern Colorado—the Durango & Silverton and the Cumbres & Toltec—and it is much shorter, so you need not relinquish a full day. Completed in 1884, the route travels four and a half miles to cover the two-mile distance between Georgetown and Silver Plume, gaining 638 feet in the process. It also traverses one of the more remarkable railroad sights in the West: the three-hundred-foot-long Devil's Gate High Bridge, where the route passes almost a hundred feet above its own tracks below.

Even if you decide not to ride the railroad, at least drive out to the Georgetown end to see the impressive bridge through Devil's Gate. Occasionally, when the steam engines are being serviced, a vintage diesel engine from the 1940s pulls the train

In addition, if you haven't toured a mine, consider adding the Lebanon Silver Mine Tour for a slightly increased cost. Mine tours in other parts of the state routinely cost twice the price of the Lebanon, but you cannot tour the Lebanon mine without taking the Georgetown train. This tour is unusual in that when the mine was abandoned in the 1890s, it was left with its machinery intact. As a result, the Lebanon remains like a time capsule of a rather primitive form of mining not usually seen in mine tours. The rough terrain to the mine and the route within, however, make this a poor choice for those unsure of foot.

When steam engines are being serviced, as they were for the 2008 season, a 1940s-vintage diesel engine pulls the observation cars. Here it crosses the high bridge at Devil's Gate.

SILVER PLUME

As the silver claims around Georgetown flourished, late-arriving prospectors naturally tried their luck in nearby areas. The most obvious place was farther up Clear Creek, whose placer deposits had begun the strikes at both Idaho Springs and Georgetown.

In the mid-1860s, another mining camp grew in a location beyond Georgetown as the result of that continued prospecting, and in 1870, major silver discoveries fueled a genuine bonanza. The most colorful account of the naming of the new town involves Commodore Stephen Decatur, editor of Georgetown's *Colorado Miner*. He had been shown ore samples featuring feathery streaks of silver in a plume shape. When asked what to call the new but unnamed camp, Decatur proclaimed, "The name? You've already got the name! It was written on the ore you brought me!" He rhapsodized:

> *The knights today are miners bold,*
> *Who toil in deep mines' gloom!*
> *To honor men who dig for gold,*
> *For ladies whom their arms enfold,*
> *We'll name the camp Silver Plume!*

The rich mines were in the steep canyon walls above the new camp. They were reached by trails, many of which are still visible today, zigzagging up from town.

One of those rich mines was the Pelican, discovered in 1868 by Owen Freeman. When he later became seriously ill and feared he was dying, Freeman confided the location to two friends. He later recovered, but when he visited his claim, he learned that his "friends" had somehow neglected to include his name on the ownership papers.

Silver Plume was incorporated in 1880 and within a couple of years could claim saloons, boardinghouses, butcher shops, mercantiles, fraternal lodges, a theater, a school, and Catholic and Methodist churches. With its modest frame buildings packed into narrow streets along the canyon floor, Silver Plume lacked the splendor of Georgetown. It was proudly proclaimed a "miners' town," whereas its more cosmopolitan neighbor was the home of mine owners and managers.

Many of those modest buildings disappeared on the night of November 4, 1884, when a fire started in Patrick Barrett's saloon. The flames spread down Main Street, consuming most of downtown. Devout women and children knelt in front of St. Patrick's Catholic Church and prayed for divine intervention. Although the fire seriously damaged the east wall, the church was spared. The next morning, Barrett's body was found in the ashes of his saloon.

Rebuilding began the next day. Citizens floated a bond issue for a water works and increased fire protection, including purchase of the town's first pumper, shipped from St. Louis. The business district was completely rebuilt by 1886, with saloons prevailing on the south side of Main Street while other businesses, such as the post office, barbershop, print shop, and mortuary, stood on the north side.

The prosperity of Silver Plume was short-lived. Like neighboring Georgetown, the community reeled from the blow of the Silver Crash of 1893.

Many of Main Street's false-front buildings were erected immediately after Silver Plume's disastrous fire of 1884.

WALKING AND DRIVING AROUND SILVER PLUME

You enter Silver Plume from Interstate 70 on Woodward Avenue, which features several homes and the lovely two-story 1880s New Windsor Hotel, now a private residence.

Turn left on Main Street, where you'll pass the 1875 two-cell stone jail, in service until 1915. Farther west on Main is the rebuilt pump house at Brewery Springs, so named because Otto Boche's Silver Plume Brewery and Bowling Alley once stood across the street.

At Main and Hancock is the attractive Methodist church, built in the 1880s and moved to this site in 1890. It has a very austere interior except for lovely chandeliers, each of which features six long, elegant arms supporting a light fixture. The church is still in use; when I looked in during one visit, empty champagne bottles from a recent wedding were sitting on a table.

Still farther west is the two-story, four-classroom, 1894 brick schoolhouse, where classes were last held in 1959. A sign proclaims that this school, like the one in Georgetown, is a "State of Colorado Standard School Approved Class." Today the building is the George Rowe Museum, named for an eighty-seven-year resident of Silver Plume who donated much of the memorabilia inside.

Silver Plume's business district has more than a dozen historic buildings, including the 1886 Hose Company No.1 and Town Hall, the 1904 bandstand, the 1874 St. Patrick's Church (enlarged after the 1884 fire), and the Knights of Pythias Castle Hall. The hall was moved from Brownsville, a now-vanished community west of Silver Plume, in 1895.

One poignant piece of Silver Plume's history is remembered high on a cliff west of town. There Englishman Heneage Griffin owned the Seven-Thirty Mine, so named because of the starting shift time, a generous hour later than most. The superintendent was Heneage's brother Clifford, whose tragic story is well known in the area.

Clifford's fiancée had been found dead in his room the night before their wedding, and people surmised he joined the Colorado gold rush to escape his grief. He was a reclusive person, living not in town but in a cabin at the mine, about fifteen hundred feet above Silver Plume. An accomplished violinist, Clifford often played from sunset until dark, much to the delight of the townspeople below, who would stay outdoors to listen and applaud appreciatively at his conclusion.

This Methodist church was originally equidistant between Brownsville and Silver Plume. When the former town declined as the latter boomed, the church was moved a half mile closer to Silver Plume in 1891.

The Silver Plume School was erected in 1894, a year after the great Silver Crash of 1893. The townspeople built the school to demonstrate their confidence in the long-term vitality of their community. It is now a museum.

On June 10, 1887, the distant audience heard his final note—followed by a gunshot. Miners ascended the steep trail to find him lying in a crude, rock-hewn tomb of his own digging. A suicide note asked that he be interred there. His brother erected a monument at the spot, reading, in part, "And in Consideration of His Own Request Buried Here."

To hike to the memorial, take the trail that begins from Main and Silver streets. The climb is strenuous and takes about three hours round trip. If you prefer to drive and catch a glimpse of the Griffin Memorial from below, take the south side frontage road paralleling Interstate 70 west from town. Shortly after it goes underneath the highway, pull off the roadway and look to the north up Brown Gulch beyond the old mine workings. Follow the falling water up to a huge outcropping on the right side of the gulch. On top stands the memorial.

Silver Plume's cemetery is hidden from view. To reach it, take the frontage road under the interstate and behind the parking lot for the Georgetown Loop Railroad (where the relocated 1884 Silver Plume Depot stands) and up Mountain Street. This street has an officious "Road Closed—Local Traffic Only" sign, but the cemetery is open to the public. Turn left onto Paul Street, circle a turnaround, and park by a path near an old turnstile and retaining wall.

Like many large cemeteries, this one has several sections for religious and fraternal groups. Among the interesting stones is a large monolith with the inscription "Sacred to the memory of Ten Italians, victims of an avalanche February 12th, 1899, erected by the public." Other Italian graves are nearby, some inscribed in Italian.

I was touched by three virtually identical markers for Stella Roberts, Olwen Roberts, and Anna Laura Roberts. None reached four years of age. Anna Laura drowned at two years and three months. Each had different mothers and fathers. I wondered if the fathers were all brothers.

WHEN YOU GO

Silver Plume is 2.2 miles west of Georgetown on Interstate 70.

FAIRPLAY'S SOUTH PARK CITY

When prospectors came to the early South Park diggings at Tarryall, a now-vanished mining camp, they found miners there in no mood to share and so nicknamed the place Grab-all. When they moved on and found placer gold in the South Platte River, the men wanted a counter to the name Grab-all for their new diggings and decided upon Fair Play in rebuke. The post office opened in that name in the summer of 1861.

In 1869, Fair Play became South Park City, but the name lasted only five years, when it reverted to its earlier name. Fair Play became a supply and social center for area mines after placer diggings gave out, and in the 1890s, dredging of the South Platte led to a resurgence of activity that lasted well into the twentieth century. The U.S. Post Office shortened the town's name to one word in 1924. When noted ghost town author Muriel Sibell Wolle visited Fairplay in 1942, a dredge was busy two miles away. She remarked that, despite its distance from town, she could hear it "shrieking and clanging." Those dredging operations left behind extensive gravel piles along the river. They are particularly visible from the north end of town.

On the southwest end of South Park City stand (from right to left) the office of the *South Park Sentinel*, Simkins General Store, the Bank of Alma, and the J. A. Merriam Drug Store. All were brought from other towns to this location.

This schoolhouse, built in 1879, stood at Garo, now mostly a place name southeast of Fairplay on the road to Hartsel.

Fairplay's earlier name of South Park City was resurrected when a pioneer museum of that name was opened to the public in 1959, the centennial of the Pikes Peak Gold Rush. One of the West's best outdoor, living-history pioneer villages, South Park City features a remarkable collection of thirty-four buildings, seven at their original locations and the remainder moved from nearby communities. The price of admission is very reasonable.

WALKING AROUND SOUTH PARK CITY

South Park City's street scene is attractive enough, but the adventure really begins when you enter the wonderful buildings. Ghost town enthusiasts dream of finding an empty town filled with artifacts that long-ago citizens left behind. South Park City is the incarnation of that dream. Some sixty thousand items pertinent to the buildings are on display. An 1879 one-room schoolhouse, with its belfry-capped vestibule, features a complete classroom. The 1880 Bank of Alma retains its teller cages and safe. J. A. Merriam Drug Store has an astonishing array of patent remedies still in their wrappers. Rache's Place displays gambling equipment similar to what was used when it operated in nearby Alma. The 1914 Baldwin locomotive is reminiscent of the type used on the Denver, South Park & Pacific narrow gauge railroad that once served Fairplay.

WHEN YOU GO

From Silver Plume, drive west 23 miles on Interstate 70 to Frisco. Head south on Colorado Highway 9 for 10 miles to the attractive former mining town of Breckenridge.

Fairplay's South Park City is 24 miles south of Breckenridge on Highway 9.

Built in 1862, the log Park County Courthouse was originally located in the now-vanished town of Buckskin Joe. It was moved to Fairplay in 1867 when that town was granted the county seat, an honor it still holds.

Moved from Alma, Rache's Place has authentic saloon furnishings and gambling equipment from the late 1800s. Note the conveniently located potbellied stove.

LEADVILLE

Leadville is legendary for its triumphs and tragedies. In 1860, a group of prospectors discovered placer gold in what they optimistically named California Gulch. The camp they founded was also named in hopeful expectation: Oro City. The gulch gave up a few million dollars in gold before its placers played out and the people drifted away. In the late 1860s, a quartz lode was developed at the Printer Boy Mine, but again the excitement was short-lived.

In the summer of 1877, however, a real bonanza was discovered around the corner from Oro City. The strike was not gold, but silver. Leadville, named for the lead carbonate in which the ore was found, came to life two miles northwest of Oro City.

The first huge returns came from the Little Pittsburg Mine early in 1878. Its riches began the storied rise—and eventual fall—of one of Colorado's most famous citizens: Horace Austin Warner Tabor.

Tabor and his wife, Augusta, arrived in Idaho Springs early in the rush to Clear Creek. While Tabor pursued placer deposits, Augusta opened a bakery. When they later moved to Buckskin Joe (a now-vanished community north of Fairplay), Tabor worked a claim but also opened a grocery store, and his wife operated their home as a boardinghouse. Eventually Horace became the postmaster of Buckskin Joe. The couple's businesses, not their mining claims, paid their bills.

Later, they went to Oro City and then Leadville, where the Tabors again had a store. A highly respected citizen, Horace was elected Leadville's first mayor. In addition to his official duties and his store, he also occasionally grubstaked prospectors.

Among the prospectors to whom Tabor gave supplies were George Hook and August Rische, who by sheer chance (legend says they selected where to dig because it was in the shade) found a silver vein that became the Little Pittsburg. Tabor's share made him rich. From there, he seemed to make one uncanny financial investment after another until he was one of the West's wealthiest multimillionaires. He lavishly spent vast sums and financed, among other projects, Leadville's Tabor Grand Hotel and Tabor Opera House.

Elizabeth McCourt Doe was called "Baby Doe" by admiring miners in Black Hawk. A divorcée when she came to Leadville, she met Horace Tabor in an elegant restaurant. Their subsequent relationship, secret marriage, and his divorce from

A tour of Leadville's Healy House, built in 1878, shows off its lovely furnishings. Also on the grounds is the Dexter Cabin Museum.

Leadville, Colorado & Southern Railroad

On Seventh Street east of Hemlock stands the historic Colorado & Southern railroad depot, now the departure point for a scenic rail ride. This train excursion promises that you "will experience the untamed wilderness" on a route that extends north from Leadville toward the huge mine at Climax on a two-and-a-half-hour trip. Much of that wilderness is at the beginning of your ride, where you go through thick stands of trees that keep you from seeing much of anything else. The most intriguing remnant along the way is an old water tower, and eventually you do have a wonderful view down to the valley (and highway) below. But those views, for me, did not justify the time or money spent on the excursion. I talked to several of my fellow passengers, and they expressed similar sentiments.

The train is diesel-powered, unlike most major tourist lines in Colorado. In the depot's parking lot stands a beautiful 1906 locomotive that I would love to see pulling the train.

For truly spectacular scenery, I recommend taking the Route of the Silver Kings (described on page 55). Best of all, it's free.

No doubt engine No. 641, a 1906 beauty, needed its massive snowplow to negotiate winter storms.

his faithful wife, Augusta, scandalized the Colorado social scene. (Augusta was given $300,000 in the divorce settlement—a paltry sum, as the Tabors were worth an estimated $9.4 million.)

Tabor and Baby Doe lived in high style until overspending, ill-advised investments, and the 1893 Silver Crash brought them to financial ruin. They who had once reigned over Leadville left for the obscurity of Ward, a much smaller mining camp north of Central City. In 1898, Tabor was granted an appointment as Denver's postmaster. He died, destitute, the following year.

Before he died, Tabor advised Baby Doe that whatever she did, she should hold onto a Leadville mine called the Matchless (named for a popular brand of chewing tobacco). He was convinced this mine, though worthless at the time, would eventually pay off and solve the couple's financial woes. Baby Doe returned to Leadville, remembering her husband's deathbed advice, and moved into a tiny shack at the deserted and rundown Matchless operation.

Baby Doe became a proud but pathetic figure in Leadville, "paying" for necessities with worthless promissory notes to sympathetic shopkeepers and refusing the charity offered by others. In March 1935, after a particularly heavy snowstorm, people grew concerned that they had not seen her. They found her frozen body, clad in rags, on the floor of her cabin.

Incidentally, Augusta Tabor, although bitter and hurt by her divorce, carefully invested her settlement. When she died in 1895 at the age of sixty-two, she left an estate of $1.5 million, making her one of Denver's wealthiest women.

In its history, Colorado has produced more silver than any other state. Leadville alone was responsible for an astonishing one-third of that total, an estimated $113 million.

The Silver Crash of 1893 nearly doomed the city, but it hung on with the discovery of gold in the Little Jonny Mine in the 1890s. In 1901, lead and zinc production kept the town alive. During Prohibition, Leadville's countless mineshafts hid stills that supplied liquor to Denver. During World War II, the construction of Camp Hale beyond Tennessee Pass created hundreds of jobs, and for a while Leadville's hotels, boardinghouses, trailers, and even its former brothels were completely occupied. Later, molybdenum mining at nearby Climax helped the Leadville economy. Everything after 1893, however, has been stopgap. Leadville's true glory days ended more than a century ago.

The Delaware Hotel Block was constructed in 1886 by Callaway brothers William, George, and John. Named for the brothers' home state, the Delaware Hotel still receives guests.

WALKING AND DRIVING AROUND LEADVILLE

Leadville for years was a rather seedy place that tourists drove through en route to fashionable destinations such as Aspen and Vail. It has improved considerably, but Leadville retains just enough tarnish that it's a delight to prowl around.

The visitors' center, on Harrison Avenue at the north end of the business district, offers several brochures to help you enjoy Leadville. The nearby Heritage Museum, located in the 1904 Carnegie Library, is a good place to start a tour of the town because it has an easy-to-follow history of Leadville with a sequential display of dioramas, photographs, and text.

One block west of the museum is the old high school, now the Mining Museum Hall of Fame. Some fine displays include the Gold Rush Room, the Blacksmith Shop, and the "underground" mine tunnels.

A block north of the two museums is the lovely Healy House, an elaborate 1878 clapboard home complete with posh Victorian furniture and antique household items.

Many historic buildings stand along the highway that passes through Leadville. The road is called Harrison Avenue, named for founding father Edwin Harrison, president of a refining and smelting company.

The Tabor Opera House, located on Harrison near Third Street, is a building not to miss. Constructed in 1879 in a mere hundred days, it was set for demolition in 1955. It was saved when Florence Hollister and her daughter Evelyn Furman bought it and began preservation of the structure. Both have since died, but the restoration continues with an active preservation foundation.

The opera house, open daily except Sundays in the summer, is an enchanting place to visit as you explore the backstage, dressing rooms, and even the balcony. When you venture onto the stage, you will be standing where legendary performers such as Oscar Wilde, Harry Houdini, and John Philip Sousa once stood.

The Western Hardware Company is on the corner of Harrison and Fifth. Inside, you'll find lots of antique items, including some mementos from Camp Hale. The antique storage bins and ornate display cases filled with old-time knickknacks are worth the visit. (Many items are not for sale, however.) Be sure to go upstairs to see where lodgers once lived and where more quirky merchandise is on display.

The east side of town contains several commercial and public buildings, including false-front stores on the northeast corner of Sixth and Poplar. At

Seventh and Poplar is the Annunciation Catholic Church, constructed over a period of years beginning in 1879. Its off-center bell tower is said to have the highest spire in the country, beginning as it does at ten thousand feet elevation.

Another interesting building is the imposing 1879 hospital, located at Tenth and Hemlock, which was operated by the Sisters of Charity. It closed in the 1960s but has been remodeled into a condominium building.

If you are interested in the saga of the Tabors, the Matchless Mine, located about a mile east of town on Seventh, is an important stop. You can stand where the body of the penniless Baby Doe was found, still heeding her deceased husband's advice to hold on to the Matchless. I found the experience quite moving. Baby Doe, incidentally, was not buried in Leadville but next to her husband in Denver.

To reach the cemeteries of Leadville, go west on Eighth from Harrison. Turn right at James, then left at the fork in the road. At Tenth and James, you will see the Evergreen Cemetery.

This cemetery, like most of the larger ones in the West, is sectioned off. A sign directs you to areas for Masons, Elks, Odd Fellows, the Ancient Order of United Workmen, and a poignant section called Baby Land.

To visit the St. Joseph Catholic Cemetery, drive west from Evergreen Cemetery on Tenth. Turn right at McWethy; the cemetery will be on your left.

Note: A quaint schoolhouse, the only historic remnant of Malta, is about four miles southwest of Leadville on U.S. Highway 24.

WHEN YOU GO

Leadville is 24 miles southwest of Interstate 70 on Colorado Highway 91. By paved road, Fairplay and Leadville are 66 miles apart via Colorado Highway 9, Interstate 70, and Highway 91.

In addition, two famous four-wheel-drive routes, over Mosquito Pass and Weston Pass, connect Fairplay and Leadville in far fewer miles. I have driven Weston Pass and ridden it on a mountain bike and know that it is for high-clearance motor vehicles only. Mosquito Pass, by reputation, is much more rugged. Inquire locally before attempting either pass.

The Route of the Silver Kings

A highly readable and informative brochure that is available at many locations in Leadville, but most assuredly at the visitors' center, leads you on an almost eighteen-mile tour up into the mine-pocked hills that stoked the riches of Leadville. A passenger car will suffice for some of the tour, but if you want to get to the most dramatic places, you will need a high-clearance vehicle. My tour, complete with stops for photographs, took just under an hour and a half.

The tour begins on the south end of Leadville at Monroe Street, which, when I went, lacked a street sign. It is the turn to the east just before the main highway veers from north-south and heads west.

You'll go up through California Gulch, where the first strikes were found, and into locales that once were vibrant communities: Oro City, Finn Town, Evansville, and Stumptown. The higher you climb, the more dramatic the views, culminating in an astonishing panorama at the Venir Shaft, which offers a view down to now-distant Leadville and across to Turquoise Lake and the Mount Massive Wilderness.

Venir Shaft.

2
COLORADO
PIKES PEAK
OR BUST

ALTHOUGH THE GOLD RUSH OF 1859 WAS KNOWN FOR THE MOTTO "PIKES PEAK OR BUST," the early discoveries were actually sixty miles northwest of that mountain. More than thirty years later, prospectors made a serious attempt to ascertain what lay practically in Pikes Peak's shadow. The reminders of the resulting bonanza are showcased at Victor, one of Colorado's best urban ghosts. Nearby is its sister bonanza town, Cripple Creek, now a lively casino town but once nearly a ghost itself.

Farther west of Victor stands charming St. Elmo, perhaps my favorite Colorado ghost town. And northwest of St. Elmo is unusual Marble, not a mining town at all but rather a place whose quarried marble gave America some of its most famous monuments. Finally, at Crystal, next to Marble, stands Colorado's most photographed structure: the hydroelectric generating plant for the mill of the Sheep Mountain Tunnel Mine.

The hydroelectric power generator building for the Sheep Mountain Tunnel Mill (now a pile of rubble) is one of Colorado's most famous ghost town structures.

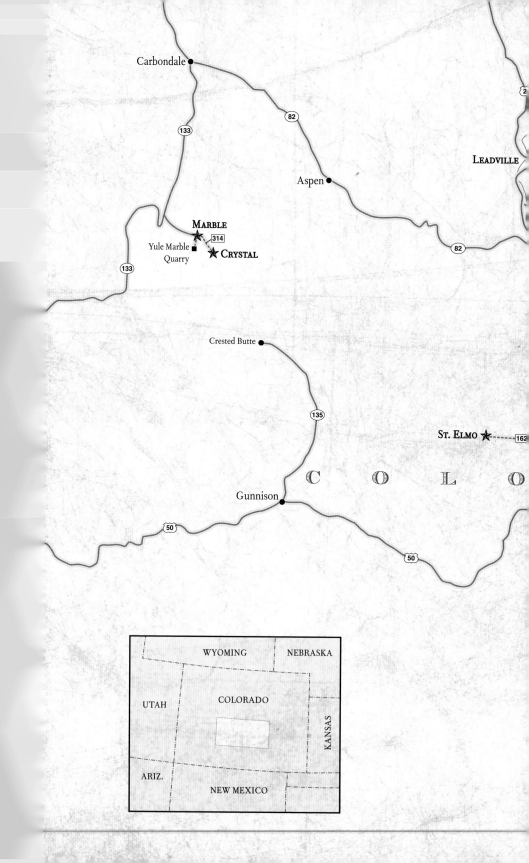

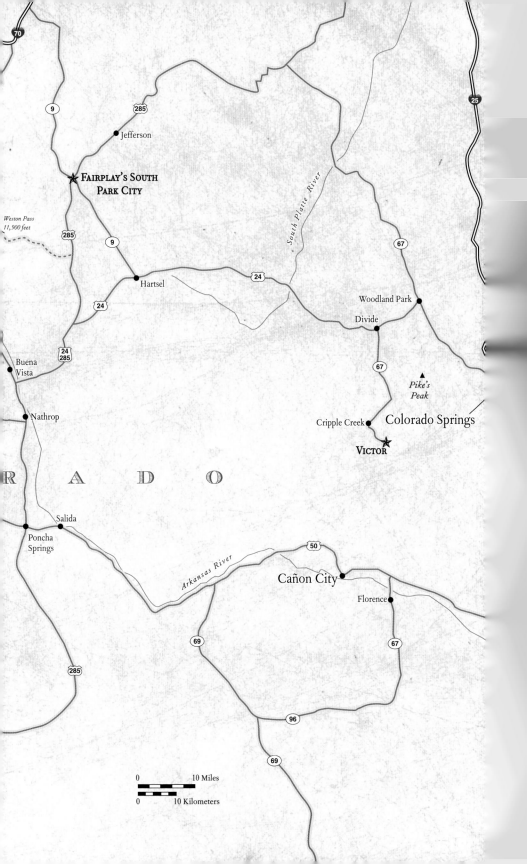

VICTOR

Victor and its more glamorous sister, Cripple Creek, practically saved Colorado. When the state was reeling from the Silver Crash of 1893, Cripple Creek and Victor were alive and thriving because gold, not silver, surrounded the towns.

Victor and Cripple Creek share much in common with Central City and Black Hawk (see chapter 1, pages 22-27). Both sets of towns were rivals and shared much of their history. All four were ghosts in the 1950s, and three of the four were rejuvenated by limited-stakes gambling beginning in 1991. Only Victor was unaffected, and for that ghost town enthusiasts can rejoice. Cripple Creek hasn't been altered as much as Black Hawk, but it nevertheless has huge, modern casinos. Because Victor was overlooked in the gambling rush, it has a somnolent, decaying beauty that the other three lack. It is, for me, one of the West's best ghost towns.

Cripple Creek's colorful name supposedly came from a mishap involving a cowboy on horseback chasing a cow into a creek, resulting in a broken leg to the horse and the cow and a broken arm to the cowboy. On hearing the account, a wag was supposed to have remarked, "That is a Cripple Creek."

Victor's name had more prosaic beginnings. It was either named for the nearby Victor Mine or for homesteader Victor Adams.

The *Victor Daily Record* newspaper was printed in the single-story brick building on the right. Next door is the triple-corniced Masonic Hall. Both buildings stand on Victor's Fourth Street.

Prospectors began to explore the Cripple Creek–Victor area in 1874, but little was found. This wasn't a place where gold should appear. The geology seemed wrong, and the deposits were hard to extract. The place confounded prospectors, confused miners, and bankrupted speculators. In 1884, a local scam brought investors to salted claims. As a result, the hills around Mount Pisgah had a tainted reputation.

The area became better known for its ranching an included property owned by Horace Bennett and Julius Myers. When prospectors once again tried the Mount Pisgah District in 1891, Bennett and Myers platted a town near the claims, named the two main streets after themselves, and named the town itself after explorer John C. Frémont.

A rival community, Hayden Placer, grew near Fremont, but ultimately the two joined, choosing the name everyone was using already: Cripple Creek. A bonanza was forecast.

Bob Womack, the original owner of Bennett and Myers' ranch, is credited with finding the first promising ore, though he reportedly sold out his claims for a few hundred dollars before the true jackpots were discovered. Another sometime Cripple Creek prospector, Colorado Springs carpenter Winfield Scott Stratton, persisted in his search for the major lode. He found it southeast of Cripple Creek on Battle Mountain, near where Victor now stands, where he made the Independence claim on July 4, 1891. He became a multimillionaire from the gold strike even as "Silver King" Horace Tabor was losing everything in Leadville.

Cripple Creek and Victor boomed as silver towns floundered. Fortunately for laid-off silver miners, they could be gold miners as well, and they were Cripple Creek–bound.

By 1894, Cripple Creek was approaching city status with electricity, telegraph service, telephones, and a population of six thousand. The mines had produced five million dollars in gold as improved technology assisted in processing ore. Another boost came that year with the arrival of the Florence & Cripple Creek Railroad, followed a year later by the Midland Terminal Railroad. Not only could ore be more efficiently processed, it could be more cheaply shipped.

Victor's Gold Coin Club still has residents. In its heyday it could boast of a library, a bowling alley, and a swimming pool.

Victor and Cripple Creek became natural rivals. Cripple Creek was home to investors and mine owners, while Victor was a miners' town. Victor, therefore, enjoyed any chance for one-upmanship. For instance, in 1897, Victor entered a float in a Salt Lake City festival with the queen of Victor aboard. She generously invited the Cripple Creek queen to ride as well. The *Victor Daily Record* wryly noted, "We might say that Cripple Creek took a ride on Victor's band wagon, but Cripple has often done that commercially and the habit is growing."

Victor even surpassed its rival in size for a short time but only because of a fire in Cripple Creek in 1896. When Cripple Creek rebuilt, however, it was again larger and even grander. When a fire decimated Victor in 1899, it also rebuilt, but its best times were already over.

In 1900, the mining district hit its peak in gold production at eighteen million dollars, when Cripple Creek was Colorado's fourth-largest city. The Cripple Creek and Victor bonanza became the second-largest gold district in U.S. history, with about twenty-one million ounces of gold extricated, worth over ten billion in today's dollars. And it is not finished, at least at this writing. An open pit operation that began in 1995 on Battle Mountain is chewing into many legendary mines, which will add to the gold-production total. Unfortunately, it is also chewing into some old mining camps.

Even though Victor was always outshone by its more genteel neighbor, the town was something special in its prime. The Portland Mine was "Queen of the District," producing half of Battle Mountain's gold. One of its muckers was a kid named William Dempsey, later famous as a heavyweight boxer under his brother's name, Jack.

Ore was found all around Victor and even within the city itself. The workings were so rich that supposedly worthless tailings were used to pave Victor's streets. When Harry Woods and his brother Frank were excavating a foundation for the Victor Hotel, they discovered a rich ore body. The hotel plan was shelved, and the Gold Coin Mine opened, eventually yielding six million dollars in gold. After the Gold Coin's buildings were destroyed in the 1899 fire, the Woods brothers rebuilt the shaft house with ornate touches like stained glass windows.

The Caffery Building has an attractive cut-stone front, built on a slight diagonal, with bricks making up the other three walls.

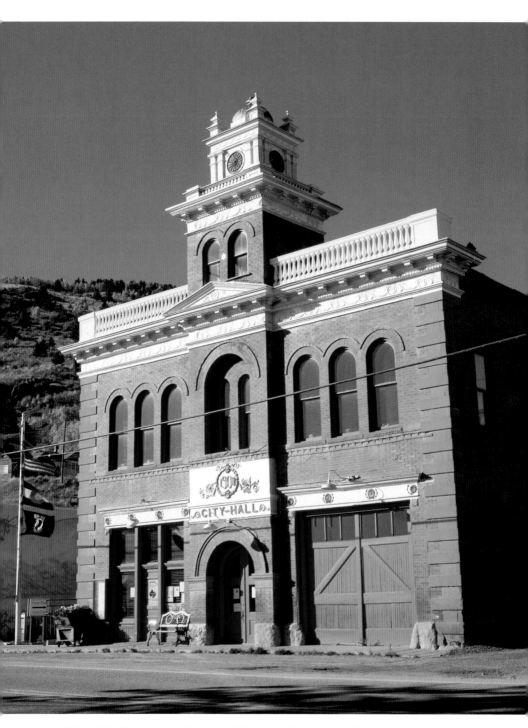

Victor's city hall features pressed-tin ornamentation and a handsome two-tiered tower

Their showy gesture demonstrated their confidence in the district. That confidence was ill-founded, however; within a few years, they were bankrupt.

Deteriorating ore bodies and labor troubles initiated Victor's decline. As a miners' town, it became the center for labor unrest when the Western Federation of Miners attempted to standardize wages and shorten the working day. Strikes and violence slowed production of nearly pinched-out mines. When miners left practically en masse to join World War I, Battle Mountain mines never recovered. The only other "mining" effort Victor saw was during the Depression, when the low-grade ore that had been used to pave the streets was scraped up and milled.

WALKING AND DRIVING AROUND VICTOR

Although Cripple Creek has succumbed to the glitter of casino gambling, Victor remains authentic—a bit dowdy, even dilapidated, but completely delightful.

Attractions for the ghost town enthusiast abound, including the Lowell Thomas Museum, on the southeast corner of Third and Victor Avenue, the main road through Victor. There you will find interesting memorabilia and items about Lowell Thomas, a Victor High School graduate whose radio voice became familiar to millions of Americans. That same intersection features the Fortune Club on the southwest corner, with an elaborate painted advertisement on its wall. South of Third from the Fortune Club is the Isis Theater, a turn-of-the-twentieth-century building that went from live theater to silent movies to talkies. Its sloping floor still has several rows of theater seats.

Farther down Victor Avenue at Fourth stands the completely renovated Victor Hotel, originally a bank. It has a huge vault in the lobby and a wonderful elevator.

South of the Victor Hotel are several outstanding buildings, including the Masonic Hall, with its three elaborate Colonial Revival cornices; the office of the *Victor Daily Record*; and the still-active First Baptist Church.

Drive the back streets south of the main business district to see countless boomtown-era homes that range from the abandoned to the neglected to the carefully restored.

North of Victor Avenue on Fourth, as you head toward the foothills of Battle Mountain, you'll see Pikes Peak Power Company Substation No. 1 on your left, and, at Fourth and Diamond, the once-elegant Gold Coin Club. Built for the workers of the Gold Coin Mine, the club featured a library, bowling alley, and

swimming pool. The mine itself, the one that was discovered while the Woods were building the foundation for a hotel, is across the street.

Continue east on Diamond and then north one block to see the Midland Terminal Railway Depot, vacant at this writing.

As you head west toward Cripple Creek, you will see another fine building on Victor Avenue: the 1900 Victor City Hall with its ornate tower. West of city hall .1 of a mile is South Seventh Street, the turnoff south to the cemetery, which is .8 of a mile away from town.

The Victor Sunnyside Cemetery has several fraternal sections: Moose, Odd Fellows, Masons, Eagles, and Elks. It also features a large number of wooden markers surrounded by wrought-iron fences.

Note: The Mollie Kathleen Mine Tour, one of the best mine tours in Colorado, is north of Cripple Creek on Colorado Highway 67. On your tour, you actually descend a thousand feet in a double cage, just as the miners did. On no other mine tour in the country can you do that.

The stone and wrought-iron Elks Rest entrance leads to that fraternal organization's section of Victor's Sunnyside Cemetery.

Opposite: Aspens signal the fall season at Sunnyside Cemetery, located southwest of Victor.

WHEN YOU GO

To reach Cripple Creek from Colorado Springs, take Colorado Highway 24 west for 25 miles to Divide. Go south 18 miles on Colorado Highway 67. Victor is 6 miles southeast of Cripple Creek on Highway 67. Incidentally, there once was another way to get from Cripple Creek to Victor: Battle Mountain is so extensively tunneled that one could actually walk between the two cities completely underground.

ST. ELMO

St. Elmo is what many people picture when someone says "ghost town." With its gorgeous scenery and attractive buildings, it's one of Colorado's premier ghost destinations.

Originally, the townsite that grew along Chalk Creek in 1879 was aptly called Forest City for the numerous spruce and pine trees in the area. But the post office refused the name, since a Forest City already existed in California. A committee of three chose St. Elmo (the patron saint of sailors) because of a popular 1866 novel of that name.

Silver and gold strikes in the Chalk Creek Mining District early in 1880 brought hundreds of people to St. Elmo. The town became a supply center for nearby mines and a jumping-off point for prospectors heading over passes to boomtowns such as Tincup and Aspen.

When the Denver, South Park & Pacific Railroad was completed to St. Elmo, the town's future seemed assured. It became a favorite place for miners, freighters, and railroad workers to spend their Saturday nights, as they enjoyed St. Elmo's many saloons.

Because of the travel trade, the town had five hotels. One guest, upon arriving at a hotel that was still getting its finishing touches, asked for a private room. The hotelier drew a chalk line around one of many beds and told him that he had given him a suite.

The failure of one mine after another and the closing of the railroad's Alpine Tunnel in 1910 began the decline of St. Elmo. The Stark family, who owned the first house in town, remained after all others left. Muriel Sibell Wolle fondly recalls Mr. Stark in her classic book *Stampede to Timberline: The Ghost Towns and Mining Camps of Colorado.* She said he was very gracious, insisting upon bringing her an armchair while she sketched. When she left his store in the otherwise-empty town, he warned, "Watch out for the streetcars!" She does not identify him except as Mr. Stark, but it was brothers Roy and Tony, along with their sister Annabelle, who ran the store until the late 1950s. After Wolle's book came out in 1949, the Starks criticized her for daring to call St. Elmo a ghost town and blamed her for their lack of business.

St. Elmo today has more than forty antique structures. As you enter town, you'll pass two restored buildings, the Pawnee Mill's livery stable and its

St. Elmo, with its dirt streets and wooden boardwalks, has the true look of a ghost town.

blacksmith shop. A house across the street is the information center for the Colorado Historical Society.

The current center of activity is the Miners Exchange, a log building with a frame false front, where you can purchase all manner of Colorado and ghost town merchandise. Perhaps the most enjoyable item to buy is food for the insatiable chipmunks that cadge snacks from visitors.

Down the street is an authentic reconstruction of the town hall and jail, which burned in 2002 along with two other buildings. Across the street is the Stark Brothers Store and sixteen-bedroom Home Comfort Hotel, built around 1885 and closed to the public at this writing. The store also housed the post office, telephone exchange, and telegraph. Attached to the Stark store (in an architecturally creative fashion) is the 1881 Heightley Cottage.

The road to Tincup Pass heads north from town. Take that road to see the completely restored 1882 one-room schoolhouse; then follow the road as it turns west to view two stores and several residences. Beyond St. Elmo, the road to Tincup Pass is for four-wheel-drive, high-clearance vehicles only.

WHEN YOU GO

St. Elmo is 24 miles southwest of Buena Vista, which is 90 miles northwest of Victor. From Buena Vista, drive south about 8.5 miles to Nathrop on U. S. Highway 285. South of Nathrop only .3 of a mile is Road 162. Take that road west for 15.4 miles to St. Elmo. The road is an old railroad grade and is suitable for passenger vehicles in good weather.

The Stark Brothers Store and Comfort Hotel is a false-front classic of the American West. Note how a second-story roof addition connects it to the adjoining Heightly Cottage.

MARBLE

"The Marble Capital of the United States" was initially settled by prospectors who formed a camp known as Yule Creek, named for pioneer George Yule. Gold, silver, and lead were mined there from 1880 into the 1890s.

Even before the prospectors found their deposits, geologist Sylvester Richardson had noted in 1873 the beds of marble in Whitehouse Mountain. The marble was merely a curiosity then, because it was on the Ute Reservation.

After the Utes were moved west to allow prospectors in, attempts to quarry the stone in the 1880s resulted in limited profitability because of the area's remoteness from a railhead. That changed when the standard gauge Crystal River & San Juan Railroad was completed from Carbondale to Marble in 1906, connecting Marble's finishing mill with the Denver & Rio Grande branch line to Aspen. That rail link, combined with a four-mile-long electric railway that transported marble from the quarry to the huge finishing mill, made production much more lucrative. The first large order, for a Cleveland, Ohio, courthouse, invigorated the community.

The best years followed, peaking from 1912 to 1917. The town was, literally, made by and of marble. Entire buildings were constructed of it, as were foundations and even sidewalks.

The town of Marble had its share of setbacks. A fire in 1916 destroyed much of downtown. Avalanches buried the finishing mill and the railroad tracks. Financial problems forced the closure of the quarry in 1941, as consumers began to order veneers instead of blocks or to choose cheaper marble substitutes. Mudslides in that year destroyed large portions of the town's business section. Machinery, rails, even metal window frames were salvaged for scrap during World War II. Its glory days apparently over, Marble became a town of pleasant summer cabins.

The quarry reopened in 1990, when the first new block of marble in almost fifty years was brought down to Marble itself, causing a "Block Party."

WALKING AND DRIVING AROUND MARBLE

When you come to a stop sign in Marble, you're in central downtown at Park and Third streets. A right turn takes you to the town's major attraction, the ruins of the Yule Quarry Finishing Mill, where blocks were cut, polished, and carved into everything from monuments to building blocks to tombstones. Exploring this

This octagon, according to the mill site tour brochure, was to be turned into a column cap, but the work was never completed.

enchanting place, for which a donation is requested, is like wandering through an Indiana Jones adventure—an ancient city with its marble pillars, brushy overgrowth, and occasional quarry blocks. One finished slab is a huge octagon about six-and-a-half feet high that looks like a sacrificial stone from some primitive civilization.

Downtown Marble is quietly alive with a bed-and-breakfast inn, a general store, several residences, galleries featuring marble sculptures, and a museum housed inside the old high school—a wooden building with a marble foundation and marble columns on its porch. The museum is located on Main west of Third Street. There you will find a pamphlet of a self-guided walking tour that directs you to the town's attractions.

One curious place nearby is at the southeast corner of Park and Third streets. It is an RV park with marble pieces standing in a bewildering assortment of shapes. It looks rather like a graveyard in which the headstones were carved by Salvador Dali.

Farther east is the Marble Community Church, moved from Aspen in 1908 on a railroad flat car. The graceful bell tower was added in 1912. The Marble City State Bank Building is on Main near First Street, and beyond it are some attractive residences. Farther east is the Beaver Lake Lodge, which features accommodations including old quarry workers' cabins. East of the lodge is Thompson Park, where Marble's two-cage jail sits. Beyond the park is Beaver Lake and the four-wheel-drive-only road to Crystal.

You pass the Marble Cemetery on your way into town. It is on the north side of the road 2.2 miles west of the intersection of Park and Third. As you would expect, most markers are indeed made of marble. One of the most attractive is a tall column back in a corner of the cemetery. The largest stone is a particularly well-carved Woodmen of the World marker that features five stacked logs for John Franklin Clayton, who died in 1911.

WHEN YOU GO

Aspen, a former mining town, later a near-ghost town, and now a world-class ski destination, is 63 miles from Buena Vista and 59 miles from Leadville over spectacular Independence Pass on Colorado Highway 82.

From Aspen, drive northwest on Highway 82 for 30 miles to Carbondale. Turn south on Colorado Highway 133 and proceed south for 21.9 miles. Turn east on Gunnison County Road 3 and go 5.9 miles to downtown Marble.

COLORADO

The Marble Community Church stands invitingly open on a lovely summer day. Inside is an operating pump organ.

Yule Marble Quarry

Yule Quarry marble is considered the finest in the United States because it is almost pure white, and it can be quarried in remarkably huge blocks. It was used for the Lincoln Memorial, the Washington Monument, and the Tomb of the Unknowns. For the latter, only this quarry could produce the fifty-six-ton slab required.

When I first visited Marble in 1987, the Yule Quarry was closed and without a barrier denying access. We took the old road up and stared at the piles of marble strewn along the way, with huge slabs creating artificial waterfalls along Yule Creek. Near the entrance to the quarry itself was a mass of marble rubble that dwarfed us. Looking inside the quarry from two vantage points, we peered into an alabaster monolithic city with sculptured walls and pillars sitting in a blue-green lagoon. Ropes, pulleys, and fragmented wooden ladders clung to the marble walls. It was midsummer, yet the water had places where the sun had neglected it, and it had frozen—not universally frozen, but solid in the shapes of the surrounding marble cliffs, etched in straight lines and parallelograms.

When I revisited Marble in 1997, the quarry was open and the road was blocked. On my most recent visit, in 2008, the road up was open to the public, even though the quarry is still active. I couldn't wait to peer into that chasm again.

The parking area for the quarry is 3.1 miles from the bridge crossing the Crystal River at Marble. It took me about a half hour from the parking area (elevation 9,116 feet) to make the uphill climb to the quarry (elevation 9,580 feet). A modest fee is requested to cross private land to reach the quarry. You will climb alongside cascading Yule Creek, where those tons of apparently inferior quality marble still form those dramatic waterfalls.

Eventually, the trail leaves creek side and you will climb a very steep slope (at one point with the aid of ropes left at the site) to the old upper entrance.

I was gazing into the quarry from the same vantage point as twenty-one years before. But the water had been drained from the workings, and heavy equipment waited at the bottom for its next load of marble. The ropes, pulleys, and ladders that I had seen before were gone, but the sight remained entrancing. If you go to Marble, and if you are physically able, take the trek up to the quarry. And it is so much easier heading back down.

Right: The Yule Quarry in 1987.

CRYSTAL

The sign east of Marble indicates four-wheel-drive vehicles only to Crystal. Heed that warning. When I first saw Crystal in 1987, I was on a mountain bike, so I wasn't too concerned about the road. The next time, in 1997, I was in my truck and glad to have another fellow explorer in a second vehicle as we slipped and slogged our way to Crystal the day after a thunderstorm. Even in dry conditions, the route would have been tricky. In 2008, I took a Jeep tour with a driver who makes the journey all summer long (inquire in Marble). The road was noticeably worse than when I drove in, and I was glad to have an expert at the wheel.

If you are a collector of books on Colorado, you will immediately recognize the first sign of Crystal: the remains of what is called the Crystal Mill, perched dramatically on a rocky crag.

Everyone says this structure is the Crystal Mill, but it really isn't. When Muriel Sibell Wolle made a drawing of the 1892 Sheep Mountain Tunnel Mill in 1947, her sketch shows a dilapidated mill standing next to this building. Caroline Bancroft has a photo from 1954 with that same mill in ruins. What remains is not the mill itself but the hydroelectric power generator, last used in 1916, for that now-vanished mill. Inside the vertical wooden shaft, which you can still see extending from the powerhouse, was a wooden water wheel that powered an air compressor for the mill.

The town of Crystal is .2 of a mile beyond the "mill." One look at the clear river water running through the valley and you might surmise how Crystal got its name. But you would be mistaken. It was not named for the water but rather for the silver-bearing quartz shot with crystallite that was found by prospectors in 1880.

Seven working silver mines kept Crystal going, and a road built over Schofield Pass to Gothic and Crested Butte in 1883 helped get supplies in and ore out. A later road went to Carbondale via the route you take into town. By 1886, about four hundred people lived in the town, which had two newspapers (including one using a wonderful pun, the *Crystal River Current*), two hotels, saloons, a billiard parlor, a barbershop, and the men-only Crystal Club.

The 1893 Silver Crash nearly emptied the town, and by 1915 only eight people lived there. A one-year mining venture brought the population up to seventy-five the next year, but after its failure, the town became deserted.

The sign is getting more and more faded on the men-only Crystal Club, one of several buildings and residences still standing from Crystal's heyday.

Crystal today contains about a dozen old cabins and the Crystal Club, made of stout logs except for the refinement of a lumber false front.

East of Crystal .3 of a mile, sitting in a ravine to your left, is the old school-house. The road eventually ascends Schofield Pass, which I have not attempted in a motorized vehicle, but I did ride on a mountain bike. On that occasion, the road was closed, and a large snowfield (in mid-July!) caused us to portage our bikes.

WHEN YOU GO

Crystal is 5.9 miles east of downtown Marble on Forest Service Road 314, the only road east from Marble.

3

COLORADO

G H O S T S   O F   T H E

SAN JUAN MOUNTAINS

THE SAN JUAN MOUNTAINS ARE SOME OF THE MOST SPLENDID IN COLORADO. Although they lack the proliferation of "Fourteeners" that the Rockies can claim (of fifty-three 14,000-foot peaks in Colorado, only thirteen are found in the San Juans), these mountains have a drama, a spectacle, that is unique in the state.

Perched near the San Juan's pinnacles and nestled in its valleys are some of Colorado's most beautiful mining camps. The ghost towns in this chapter range from deserted Carson, Summitville, Animas Forks, and Alta to busy but charming tourist towns Lake City, Creede, and Silverton. In addition, the area features an excellent mill tour, the best mining tour I've ever taken, and the world-famous Durango & Silverton Narrow Gauge Railroad.

The person whose history connects almost every site in this chapter is Otto Mears. He came to the United States a Russian orphan in 1850 at age ten, and a year later he was in the California Gold Rush. A small man with towering energy, Mears later served in the Civil War, fought Indians under Kit Carson, and learned to speak the language of the Ute Indians fluently. In Colorado, he became known as the "Pathfinder of the San Juans" for his ability to create a road where others could not.

The Duncan House in Animas Forks is one of southwestern Colorado's most photographed buildings.

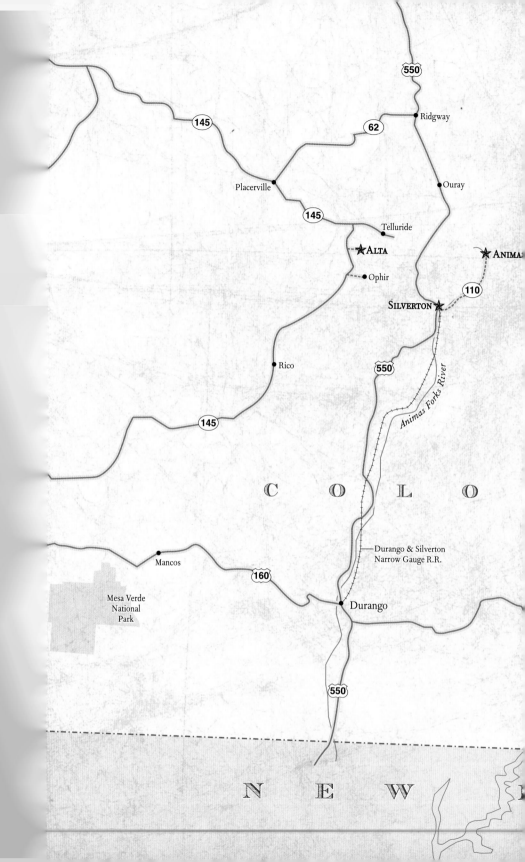

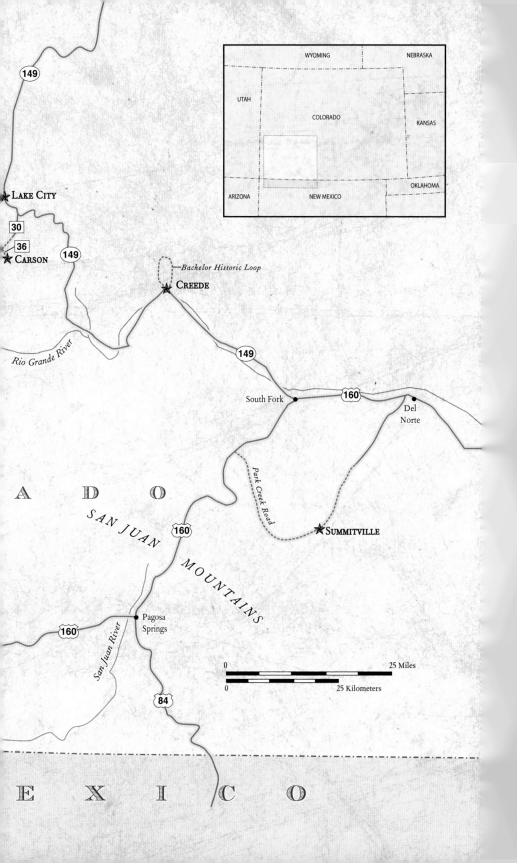

149

LAKE CITY

30
36
CARSON   149

Bachelor Historic Loop
CREEDE

149

Rio Grande River

South Fork   160

Del
Norte

WYOMING   NEBRASKA

UTAH

COLORADO

KANSAS

ARIZONA   NEW MEXICO   OKLAHOMA

A   D   O

SAN JUAN

160

Park Creek Road

SUMMITVILLE

M
O
U
N
T
A
I
N
S

Pagosa
Springs

160

San Juan River

84

0   25 Miles

0   25 Kilometers

E   X   I   C   O

LAKE CITY

Lake City rivals Georgetown as one of Colorado's most charming communities. Although smaller than Georgetown and not quite as splendid, it is also not nearly as crowded or tourist-oriented. Its downtown has some delightful buildings, while residential areas feature attractive homes and churches.

The region's most infamous incident occurred in late 1873 or early 1874, before Lake City existed. Alferd Packer was hired by Utah prospectors to guide them through the San Juan Mountains. Many gave up as winter approached, but five men continued with Packer. Two months later, when he arrived, alone, at Los Pinos Indian Agency, Packer claimed he had become separated from his companions and had nearly starved.

A search party found the men near Lake San Cristobal. All were dead, four from ax blows, the fifth from a bullet. All had been, literally, butchered. Remembering that the "nearly starved" Packer had seemed suspiciously well fed, the would-be rescuers reached a logical but grisly conclusion. By the time the search party returned, Packer had vanished.

Meanwhile, other prospectors were also combing the San Juans. The area's mineral deposits were spotted in 1874 by surveyor Enos Hotchkiss while scouting a wagon route through the San Juans. He and his party abandoned the road project and spent the winter staking claims.

By the spring of 1875, a camp of four hundred citizens was firmly established where Hotchkiss' party had settled. Hotchkiss returned to road-building long enough to create a toll road from Saguache with partner Otto Mears.

Improved roads meant cheaper transportation of ore, and the camp, called Lake City for Lake San Cristobal, boomed. Also in 1875, the town wrested the seat of recently created Hinsdale County from San Juan City, which has since disappeared.

The arrival of the Denver & Rio Grande Railroad in the late 1880s added to Lake City's status. The town could boast of its five general stores, five saloons, three restaurants, three breweries, two drugstores, two bakeries, two blacksmith shops, two meat markets, a newspaper, and a public library.

Back to unfinished business. In 1883, nine years after he had been suspected of murder and cannibalism, Alferd Packer was apprehended in Wyoming and brought to Lake City for trial. When Packer had left his camp near Lake San

Lake City's Silver Street has several excellent examples of wooden commercial buildings. Each features an attractive cornice atop its false front.

First Baptist Church's graceful off-center steeple and pretty stained-glass windows make it one of Lake City's most attractive places of worship.

Cristobal, there was no Lake City; less than a decade later, he was being tried in its two-story courthouse. He was found guilty of murder and sentenced to death, but the sentence was later reduced to a prison term. After serving several years, Packer was paroled.

The Silver Crash of 1893 damaged Lake City, but enough gold was also being mined that the town held on into the twentieth century.

WALKING AND DRIVING AROUND LAKE CITY

At the south end of Lake City's business district, at Silver and Second streets, is the Hinsdale County Museum. It is housed in the Finley Block, a single-story stone building constructed by stonemason Henry Finley, who fashioned the attractive storefront himself.

The museum has many unusual items and displays. For example, one exhibit features Susan B. Anthony's visit to Lake City in 1877; another shows a dollhouse made by Alferd Packer while he was in prison. One exhibit showcases the Hough Firefighters, which were sponsored by John Simpson Hough, a prosperous entrepreneur. His backing of the fire department was a public-spirited thing to do—and practical, because the firefighters protected his investments as well as those of others.

Downtown Lake City features several other historic buildings. At the corner of Silver and Third stands the 1877 Stone Bank Block, which served as a bank until 1914. It was then converted to other uses, including a forty-year stint as a hotel. Around the corner is Armory Hall, originally the opera house, built in 1883. The restricted, posh Hinsdale Club for men used the building's second floor.

The Hough Block, on the east side of Silver in the next block north, was built by John Hough between 1880 and 1882. For Lake City old-timers, however, the block is remembered for Mike and Stella Pavich, who purchased the building in 1932 and ran Mike's Place Cafe until 1945, when they turned it into a grocery.

The 1877 Hinsdale County Courthouse is one block east of the highway between Third and Fourth streets. The first-floor corridor displays documents on the Alferd Packer trial. The second-floor courtroom, except for a microphone and computer, transports you to 1877.

Too many historic residences stand in Lake City to enumerate them all, but here are several of my favorites. At the northeast corner of Fifth and Gunnison (Colorado Highway 149) is the 1877 John Hough House. Across the street is the small 1876 St. James Episcopal Chapel, originally a carpentry shop. South of the chapel is the lovely 1877 Turner House at 513 Gunnison. (Turner and a partner operated the carpentry shop that later became the chapel.)

The most grandiose residence in town, the 1892 Youmans House, stands on the northeast corner of Sixth and Gunnison. A plaque in front of the home wryly states that the home was "intended to be noticed."

Henry Kohler's brick home stands on the northeast corner of Fifth and Silver. Kohler, a pharmacist, returned to his native Germany to get his bride and built this home for her as a wedding present.

In addition to the St. James Episcopal Chapel, three other attractive churches remain in Lake City. The Presbyterian church, built in 1876, is located on Fifth near Gunnison. The narthex and steeple were added in 1882, with side doors flanking a decorative center window. It was aesthetic, perhaps, but not practical—caskets could not get through the side doors. The window was eventually replaced with a main door that gave pallbearers a straight shot into the church.

The 1891 First Baptist Church stands on Bluff Street at Fourth. The steeple is forty-five feet high, and the church can accommodate almost two hundred worshipers.

The third church, one few visitors see, is the St. Rose of Lima Catholic Church. To reach it, cross Henson Creek Bridge on the south side of town. In deference to the residents of the Henson Creek RV Park, leave your car on Gunnison and walk rather than drive through their park. The church was built in 1878 and restored between 1982 and 1992. Beyond it stands a handsome mansard-roofed brick home.

South of town 2.8 miles on Highway 149 is the Alferd Packer Massacre Site. Five metal crosses mark where Israel Swan, George Swan, Frank Miller, James Humphreys, and Wilson Bell were murdered.

The Lake City Cemetery is located a mile north of downtown along the highway. Another cemetery is a half-mile away. From the Lake City Cemetery, head north and then immediately turn left onto Balsam Drive, following the road to an attractive wrought-iron fence.

WHEN YOU GO

Lake City is 54 miles southwest of Gunnison and 52 miles northwest of Creede on Colorado Highway 149.

The Hinsdale–IOOF Cemetery has hundreds of graves. Two markers recall mining's dangers. Harry Pierce died in an explosion at the Ulay Mine in 1878. Judson Hillis died in 1890 "as a result of an accident in the Ulay Mill on Henson Creek."

A grave on a hill in the northwest corner affected me enormously. It is for Roger David Coursey, age forty-four, who "gave his life in the line of duty November 18, 1994." I was so touched by the stone and its inscriptions that I returned to the sheriff's office (located in a building dedicated to Coursey) to learn more.

Roger Coursey died ten days into his first elective term as Hinsdale County's sheriff after two men attempted to rob a bank in Creede. He and another officer stopped the men's car near the turnoff to the Packer massacre site. Sheriff Coursey was shot dead, leaving a wife and four children. A simple white cross along the highway near the Packer site marks where he died.

The Hardtack Mine Tour

The Hardtack Mine Tour, advertised in Lake City as "a real mine," is a worthwhile introduction to mining if you haven't already taken other such tours. It's a reasonable value for an approximately forty-minute tour that features lots of rusted mining equipment set up with mannequin miners. My guide's information was accurate and interesting.

The only problem is that there never was a Hardtack Mine. What you enter was originally a proposed transportation tunnel intended to move ore more quickly from the nearby Hidden Treasure Mine. After almost seven years of digging, beginning in 1899, it was abandoned, so it never was any part of a working mine.

Despite its good intentions, the Hardtack Mine Tour does not compare to two better Colorado tours mentioned in this book, the Mollie Kathleen Mine Tour (page 66) or the Old Hundred Mine Tour (page 105).

The Hardtack Mine is 2.7 miles west of Lake City on Henson Creek Road (County Road 20), the route over Engineer Pass.

CARSON

Like many other true ghost towns, Carson sits in an unspeakably beautiful setting. Like a few others, it is unoccupied. This combination makes Carson one of my favorite mining camps anywhere.

Christopher J. Carson, prospecting along the Continental Divide, found gold and silver in 1881 and staked a claim for the Bonanza King. The small camp named for Carson struggled through the early 1880s because of transportation problems, but miners still managed to work 150 claims in which silver outproduced gold by a hundred ounces to one.

Transportation woes were eased when a road coming from Lake City was begun in 1883, led by an overseer named Wager, for whom the gulch was named. Another road from Wagon Wheel Gap reached the south side of the divide in 1887.

The reliance on silver crippled Carson in 1893 when silver prices plummeted. But in 1896, promising gold deposits were found, bringing more than four hundred miners back, principally to the St. Jacobs and Bachelor mines. At this time, buildings were constructed north of the pass at a "new" Carson. "Old" Carson was on the south side. By 1902, however, the *Gunnison Times* reported, "Carson with its many promising properties is practically abandoned."

Standing at the new Carson today are seven structures, one made of logs and the others of cut lumber. Each has a sturdy metal roof, thanks to the town's owner. (Carson is private property, but it is not posted against trespassing at this writing.)

The largest building was a boardinghouse for Bachelor Mine employees and may also have served as a hospital. It is interesting architecturally because it was built as if it were three separate structures connected by hallways. The walls are covered with graffiti, one reason why sites like this become closed to the public.

Two nearby homes for the Bachelor Mine foreman and superintendent had tongue-in-groove interior woodwork, indicating that these buildings were not of slapdash construction. North of those homes is a buggy shed and stable.

The nearby Bachelor Mine is posted against trespassing, but you can see it nonetheless. Behind the Carson buildings is a faint trail that heads to the southeast. In perhaps thirty yards, you'll come out behind the mine, where, without trespassing, you can view the operation, including a boiler, cable winch, dumps, and rotting boards.

The living quarters for the mine's foreman and the superintendent have a touch of class that the other five buildings at Carson do not: tongue-in-groove interior woodwork. Unfortunately, the residences, like the others in town, are marred by graffiti.

Very little remains at old Carson, south of the Continental Divide. When Muriel Sibell Wolle hiked there in 1948, she saw mine buildings, houses, an old hotel, and the post office.

WHEN YOU GO

From Lake City, head southeast on Colorado Highway 149 for 2.3 miles to Road 30, the turnoff to Lake San Cristobal and Cinnamon Pass. Drive 9 miles to Wager Gulch Road (Road 36), which goes south. The next 3.6 miles to Carson require a four-wheel-drive vehicle, especially in wet conditions.

CREEDE

No one knew it then, but Creede would be known as The Last of the Silver Towns. The area's bonanza began in 1890, a scant three years before the Silver Crash.

"Holy Moses!" Nicholas Creede is supposed have exclaimed to his partner when he found a rich silver outcropping in 1889. He staked his claim in that name. When David Moffat, Denver & Rio Grande Railroad president, toured the Holy Moses in 1890, he bought into the mine for sixty-five thousand dollars.

When others heard that a respected man like Moffat was involved, the rush began. By the fall of 1890, houses, cabins, tents, and businesses lined Willow Creek for six miles with such density that one pioneer recalled there was not one square foot unstaked. The lots were going at prices so outrageous that crafty settlers outsmarted lot owners by extending planks across Willow Creek and erecting shacks on them. Crafty it was, until the creek rose.

Several towns evolved along Willow Creek, including two of considerable size. The original Creede, up the canyon from the present town, became known as North Creede. South of that was Stringtown, followed by the other large settlement, Jimtown, which became present-day Creede. High above Jimtown to the west was Bachelor, the largest "suburb."

The Denver & Rio Grande arrived in 1891. Each new train brought as many as three hundred people to an already overcrowded Creede. Life moved at a frantic pace. A load of lumber one day was a store the next. Just five days after a groundbreaking for a power plant, Creede had electricity. As newspaper editor Cy Warman wrote in an oft-quoted poem, "It's day all day in the day-time /And there is no night in Creede."

Floods and fires plagued Creede and Jimtown because of their locations in or near narrow, deep canyons. Mere cloudbursts sent torrents of water through both towns. A saloon fire in 1892 reduced most of Jimtown's business district to charred sticks.

In 1893, Jimtown, by then called Creede, had a reported ten thousand citizens. They took the seat of newly created Mineral County from now-vanished Wason. Legend says they seized more than the seat: Piece by piece, they moved the courthouse as well.

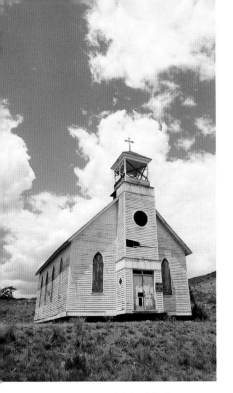

The demonetization of silver in 1893 ended Creede's bonanza, and by 1900, fewer than a thousand residents remained in Creede. Although the boom was over, significant mining continued off and on until 1985. The current population is less than four hundred.

And what became of Nicholas Creede, who began the bonanza? In 1897, he committed suicide with a morphine overdose in Los Angeles because, a contemporary report stated, "his wife, from whom he had separated, insisted on living with him."

The Creede Cemetery stands behind this Victorian Gothic-style catholic church, built around 1898, which was moved to this location in 1976. A complete restoration of the building is planned by its current owner, Creede Mining Heritage.

WALKING AND DRIVING AROUND CREEDE

Creede's 1891 railroad depot, in the middle of town on Main Street, now houses a museum that features old photographs, a hand-drawn fire truck, a hearse, gaming tables, and other interesting items, including a piano that came to Creede by wagon. The piano was last played by Chester Brubacher, who didn't read music. To fill the music stand in front of his eyes, Chester placed a Sears catalog on it. When he played happy music, he turned the catalog to women's bras. When he played a sad song, he paged over to the corset section.

Downtown Creede has several other attractive buildings, including the Creede Hotel, the tin-false-front Quiller Gallery, and a mercantile that was later the firehouse (now a bed-and-breakfast inn).

WHEN YOU GO

Creede is 52 miles southeast of Lake City and 21 miles north of South Fork on Colorado Highway 149.

The Bachelor Historic Tour

The Bachelor Historic Tour, named for the "suburb" high above and west of Creede, is one of the best scenic loops in the West. The drive requires a vehicle with reasonable power for a couple of steep grades, but in good weather a passenger car or van will certainly suffice.

You will enjoy this loop to the fullest if you use the well-written, well-illustrated booklet that is available, at a very modest cost, at the Creede Visitors' Center on Main Street.

The seventeen-mile tour begins at a display just north of downtown Creede. Because you will have that booklet, I won't duplicate the tour, except to say that you will gasp at the Commodore Mine buildings early in the loop. Another stop is at Bachelor, named for its single, male inhabitants. Today, the site shows hardly a trace of its former vitality.

The next-to-last stop on your tour loop is at the Creede Cemetery, which contains more wooden fences and markers than most Colorado graveyards.

The final stop of the tour is north of the cemetery, where Bob Ford, who gained ignominy for shooting Jesse James in the back, was buried, himself the recipient of a gunshot. His wife, however, had the body exhumed and taken to Missouri for reburial.

If you don't have time to do the entire tour, at least drive north on Main Street and visit the base of the dramatic buildings of the Commodore Mine.

Opposite: The Commodore Mine operation.

SUMMITVILLE

Summitville still hums with activity. However, it is not mining causing all the action; it is the removal of mining's detritus. Summitville is one of Colorado's several environmental Superfund sites, and the cleanup operation has been immense. When I first visited the site in 1997, the renovation was in full swing, with huge trucks hauling contaminated waste from the site. In 2008, the cleanup seemed to be in the late stages.

The ghost town of Summitville, fortunately, was not part of the decontamination area, and there remains much to see. Summitville is, however, a very vulnerable site, especially—at an elevation of 11,300 feet—to the elements, and it is a natural candidate for another kind of "superfund": preservation money from Colorado's gaming dollars.

In 1870, rancher James Esmund and a companion rode their horses into a high, parklike area in search of two runaway girls. They found the girls, and Esmund found something else: free gold in the rocks all around. He returned several times to remove high-grade ore, but he neglected to file claims.

In June 1870, a party of prospectors, including James and William Wightman, staked claims along the creek, now named for the brothers. Winter drove them out, but the next spring brought hundreds of argonauts. In 1872, hundreds more arrived, so when James Esmund returned once again, he discovered people swarming over the area, including on his find, by then known as the Little Annie. He nevertheless staked claims for the Esmund (later the Aztec) and the Major mines.

Summitville received its post office in 1876. By 1883, the town was Colorado's biggest gold producer, occupying several hundred miners and mill workers for hugely successful mines, such as the Little Annie and the Bonanza. By 1889, however, the boom was over and only a few diehards remained.

Summitville's main pump house is, unfortunately, sagging toward the horizontal. The building is well worth resurrecting because of the unusual "chimney," which was actually a passageway to enter the pump house when snow covered the normal entrance.

A short-lived rebirth came in the late 1890s with the reopening of the Bonanza, but the mine's production fizzled by 1900. Miners tried again for two years beginning in 1911, for five years starting in 1926, and for about fifteen years commencing in the 1930s.

Another attempt was beginning after World War II, when Muriel Sibell Wolle visited Summitville. She was expecting a deserted ghost town but found instead a lively company town of tarpaper-covered shacks and a large community hall flying an American flag.

Further attempts were made in the 1970s, but not even the discovery of a boulder containing $350,000 in gold lying near a road could revitalize the town.

WALKING AROUND SUMMITVILLE

If you follow my road directions, below, you'll enter Summitville from the south. The first building will be on your right, along Wightman Creek. It is the sagging main pump house, architecturally interesting because it has a "chimney" passage so that it could be entered from above when winter snow covered the normal entrance. Above the pump house stands a two-story wood-frame structure that looks like a dormitory.

The only site you can explore without violating "no trespassing" signs is also the best of the townsite, but you'll need to hike up to it. North of the road, opposite the pump house and up on a hill to the east, stand almost twenty buildings: cabins, pump houses, and outhouses. About a half dozen are partially or completely collapsed, but most are under roof.

Beyond these buildings .3 of a mile, on the south side of the road, is a cluster of about a dozen residences and outbuildings on a small hill. At this writing, the wood-frame structures are under roof, partially covered with tarpaper, and posted against trespassing. From there, the road winds down for 27 miles to Del Norte, but that road is not as smooth or wide as the route you took up. For that road, I'd recommend a truck.

Several dozen buildings, most of them miners' cabins, stand at Summitville today. The main boom only lasted from 1870 until 1889, but gold was still being extracted from its mines into the 1970s.

WHEN YOU GO

You can reach Summitville from either South Fork or Del Norte. The easier route by far is from South Fork (21 miles southeast of Creede) because the ascent to Summitville follows a haul road wide enough and level enough for huge trucks. From South Fork, head 7.1 miles southwest on U.S. Highway 160. Turn left onto Park Creek Road and follow it for 14.6 miles, where a left turn onto Forest Service Road 380 takes you in 2.2 miles to Summitville. In good weather, a passenger car should have no difficulty reaching the townsite.

SILVERTON

Among the first prospectors to reach the San Juan Mountains was a party led by Captain Charles Baker in 1860, lured by the captain's glowing accounts of a previous trip. Actual results were so meager that his disgruntled followers considered lynching him.

The area's isolation hindered exploration, but continued prospecting efforts in the 1870s brought pressure upon the federal government to "adjust" a treaty with the Ute Indians, essentially forcing them to give up the San Juans in an 1873 agreement known as the Brunot Treaty.

Two years later, a small community named Baker's Park was established in a lovely valley surrounded by silver-bearing mountains. The town was carefully platted and featured wide main streets to facilitate wagon traffic. The post office was granted to Silverton, likely a shortened version of "Silvertown." An apocryphal story, however, claims the town got its name when a miner cried out that, although they had no gold, they had "silver by the ton."

Transportation of even the richest ore created considerable obstacles for miners, because ore had to be packed out by mules, transferred to wagons at the first road, and freighted to the nearest railhead, which originally was Pueblo. The arrival of the Denver & Rio Grande from Durango in 1882 alleviated that difficulty, cutting transportation costs by 80 percent. Silverton's isolation was over—as long as the rails were clear. Snowslides in 1884, for example, forced snowbound citizens to scrape down to their last bits of food as they endured for seventy-three days before a train could get through. The rail link to Durango was the community's lifeline.

In addition to food, the railroad could bring in everything that turns a camp into a town. Silverton's Greene Street became an elegant thoroughfare, highlighted by the three-story brick Grand (later Grand Imperial) Hotel. Other commercial buildings vied for attention with attractive cornices and elaborate façades. Silverton never suffered a major fire, so the fine buildings remain intact today.

One block east stood Blair Street, so notorious for its saloons and brothels that residents at either end called their sections "Empire Street" to avoid being tainted by association.

Most of the buildings on Silverton's Greene Street date from the 1880s and 1890s. Notice the handsome cornices and inventive trim colors.

The Silver Crash of 1893 dealt a blow to Silverton, but by 1897 half of the town's ore production was for gold, followed by silver, lead, and copper. Output reached its zenith between 1900 and 1912 and continued until World War II.

The new gold arrived after World War II when the Denver & Rio Grande's spectacular railroad began to attract tourists. Now called the Durango & Silverton Narrow Gauge Railroad, the train brings about two hundred thousand people to Silverton annually.

WALKING AND DRIVING AROUND SILVERTON

Silverton's stores offer a free visitors' guide that includes a walking tour.

An appropriate place to begin is the San Juan County Museum, located at the north end of town. The museum is housed in the 1902 county jail, and much original equipment remains. The first floor features the sheriff's office and family quarters, the kitchen, and the sole women's cell. Men's cells are on the second floor, along with a door to the jail at Animas Forks (see following entry, pages 108–109).

On your way downtown, visit the 1906 San Juan County Courthouse next door to the museum. Built in a cruciform configuration, its elaborate halls dramatically lead to a single central spot: a simple drinking fountain.

South of the courthouse on Greene is the 1902 Wyman Hotel, now a bed-and-breakfast. Across the street is the handsome 1908 town hall, gutted by a 1992 fire but

Silverton's Hillside Cemetery, north of town, has hundreds of varied tombstones. Sultan Mountain is prominent in the background.

beautifully restored by 1995. When you venture inside to see its graceful staircases, you will be amazed that skeptics considered the building beyond saving after the fire.

For the next four blocks heading south from the town hall, virtually every building on the west side of Greene dates back to the nineteenth century, as do many on the east side. Even the newer buildings look authentic. Your visitors' guide will give you information on individual buildings.

Other commercial structures are found one block east of Greene on the once-notorious Blair Street. Notice the 1883 jail at the corner of Thirteenth and Blair. It was constructed by laying boards flat and stacking them log-cabin style on top of each other for strength. A similar jail stands in Animas Forks.

One block west of Greene is Reese Street, where you will find many attractive residences. In that same area are the school, Carnegie Library, and three churches.

To reach Silverton's Hillside Cemetery, go north from town to a junction of roads. Take the north road and turn right at the first opportunity. The cemetery looks down upon the picturesque town and has a sweeping view of the mountains surrounding the valley.

The oldest graves are to your left, past a small block shed near a fence. There you will find an unusual marker for Alfred Moyle, who died in 1888 at eight years of age. The stone features a child reclining on a blanket, with a clamshell spreading out protectively over him. Nearby is the cemetery's first burial plot, the 1875 grave of Rachel E. Farrow, along with the earliest headstone, for James Briggs, who died in a snowslide in 1878.

Three other interesting headstones are for William Henry Richards, who died in an 1889 Yankee Girl mining accident; for John Herbert, buried next to Richards, "accidentally hurt at Robinson Mine, Red Mountain," in 1890; and for Lewis Owen, next to Herbert, who died at the Yankee Girl in 1892.

WHEN YOU GO

Silverton is 49 miles north of Durango and 25 miles south of Ouray on U.S. Highway 550. With a four-wheel-drive, high-clearance vehicle, you can go from Lake City to Silverton over either Cinnamon Pass or Engineer Pass. I have done both on a mountain bike (with plenty of walking) but have not driven either. These roads are for serious backroad vehicles and experienced drivers only. Inquire locally as to road conditions.

The Mayflower Mill and Old Hundred Mine Tours

Not far from Silverton are the best mill and mine tours I have ever taken. To reach the Mayflower Mill and the Old Hundred Mine, drive to the north end of Silverton on Greene Street, turn right at the junction, and proceed northeast 1.9 miles to the Mayflower Mill. The Old Hundred is .5 of a mile east of the tiny ghost town of Howardsville, which is 2 miles beyond the Mayflower Mill. Signs clearly mark the way to both attractions.

Mine tours should be enjoyable for almost everybody, because they can be exciting and seem almost adventurous. Mills are different. I think you must want to know how a mill works, because a good mill tour will provide considerable information. I found the Mayflower Mill Tour fascinating.

Many mills in the West were dismantled and sold for scrap in the 1940s to aid the war effort. The Mayflower, however, operated until 1991, and all the equipment that was functioning on its last day is still in place.

Our guide, a ten-year mill employee, was informative and knowledgeable. As we walked through the mill, she told us, without unnecessarily elaborate explanations, how crude rocks were reduced to finished amalgam.

The Old Hundred Mine Tour is excellent for a number of reasons. First, the train ride in, about one-third of a mile, is short enough not to be monotonous. Second, you explore several areas featuring different mining operations and equipment. Third, some of that equipment is actually operational: Two drills and a mucker are fired up for just long enough to demonstrate that the mine certainly wasn't the silent place it is now. Finally, our tour guide was marvelous. A former miner, he could have been a siding salesman, so enthusiastic and entertaining was his pitch.

A short, beautiful side trip begins below the Mayflower Mill and crosses the Animas Forks River. In only 1.5 miles, you follow a road toward the Mayflower Mine. You'll frequently be near the towers that supported a tramway, which operated from 1930 until 1963 and transported ore from that mine to the Mayflower Mill. On occasion, you'll pass beneath the buckets suspended overhead. At road's end, you'll be creekside in magnificent Arrastra Gulch, looking up toward the mine itself.

Durango & Silverton Narrow Gauge Railroad

People come from all over the world to ride this spectacular train, and so should you. You can choose a round-trip journey from Durango to Silverton or a one-way with a bus return. If you have small children, you might prefer the latter. Otherwise, I recommend the nine-hour round trip, which includes more than an hour's layover in Silverton. The train offers four classes of travel: Presidential, First, Premium, and Standard. I have never splurged for the Presidential Class, but I have twice taken the First Class Alamosa Parlor Car (no minors allowed, because it has a bar), and I admit I'm spoiled.

A recent addition to the line, which I have not taken, is the First Class Silver Vista (for travelers ages sixteen and over), an open gondola with an elaborate glass canopy.

The Durango & Silverton is not inexpensive, but the day's memories will be worth the cost. Reservations are strongly recommended. Whether you take the train or not, if you are in Durango, consider visiting the railroad's museum, where you can climb inside a caboose and a private business coach and even take the engineer's spot in the cab of a 1902 locomotive. An outdoor viewing area allows you to watch mechanics servicing locomotives in the roundhouse and, if you are lucky, to see a locomotive on the turntable.

The train from Durango, under a full head of steam, passes the depot on its way to Silverton.

ANIMAS FORKS

North of Silverton stand the remains of three mining towns: Howardsville, Eureka, and Animas Forks. The first two, at 3.9 miles and 7.6 miles northeast of Silverton, respectively, have rather scant remains. Howardsville has the tram terminus of the Little Nation Mine and a couple of cabins. Eureka features a restored water tank, which later was modified to become a firehouse and jail, and the immense foundations of the two mills of the Sunnyside Mine.

If you are a bit disappointed with the remains at Howardsville and Eureka, you will be well rewarded by continuing north from Eureka 4.2 miles to see the considerable remnants of Animas Forks.

Personally, I will always have a special fondness for Animas Forks, given a somewhat adventurous trip I once made there. In late July 1989, several companions and I rode mountain bikes from Lake City to Silverton. At Cinnamon Pass, we hit a lightning-filled sleet storm and practically slid down to Animas Forks, where we found shelter and huddled together for warmth.

Animas Forks was founded in 1873 when prospectors built log cabins near their claims. Because three rivers met nearby, the camp was called Three Forks, or Forks of the Animas. The name was simplified to Animas Forks by the U.S. Postal Service when a post office was granted in 1875.

At almost 11,200 feet, the town suffered from severe winters. Most of the miners retreated in the fall and return the following spring. The hearty few who stayed were subjected to avalanches and isolation. In 1884, the year Silverton endured ten weeks without relief supplies, Animas Forks was snowbound for twenty-three days. Provisions had to come from Silverton, which had none to spare.

Animas Forks emptied in 1891 as mining declined. A brief resurgence occurred in 1904 with the construction of the Gold Prince Mill, which was connected to its mine by a 2.4-mile tramway. The mill caused Otto Mears to extend his Silverton Northern Railway from Eureka to Animas Forks, further raising expectations for the town. But the mill closed in 1910, and Animas Forks lost its post office in 1915. In 1917, the mill was largely dismantled for use at Eureka's Sunnyside Mill.

At this writing, ten buildings stand completely or partially under roof around the townsite. As you cross the Animas Forks River entering town, the foundations of the Gold Prince Mill will be on your right.

The William Duncan House, built in 1879, has been stabilized thanks to the attention of the San Juan County Historical Society.

One of Colorado's more photographed ghost town buildings is the 1879 William Duncan home, featuring a dramatic bay window. Historical signs at the site describe several other structures, among them the unusual jail. The jail is one of four in the area built using the same construction method: boards laid flat and stacked log-cabin style, so the structure has a stockade's strength. Similar structures stand in Silverton, Red Mountain, and Telluride. The door to this one is now housed in the museum in Silverton.

WHEN YOU GO

Animas Forks is 12 miles northeast of downtown Silverton on Colorado Highway 110. It is 8.1 miles north of the turnoff at Howardsville to the Old Hundred Mine.

ALTA

Alta (Spanish for "high") was a company town for the Gold King Mine, discovered in 1878. Alta had a general store, an assay office, a school, miners' homes, and company offices. The town also became the upper terminus for a tram that extended almost two miles and dropped more than eighteen hundred feet to Ophir Loop, where a loading bin was located near the Rio Grande Southern depot. (Ophir Loop is located 1.8 miles south of the turnoff to Alta on Colorado Highway 145.)

The Alta-area mines produced into the 1940s under the ownership of the Silver Mountain Mining Company, but a fire in one of the shafts in 1945 effectively ended production.

When I first saw Alta in 1987, it was abandoned and deteriorating. Since then, efforts have begun to preserve and protect the buildings. The Alta I first saw, if left to the elements and vandals, would be in a sorry state today.

When you enter Alta, you will be at the bottom of the townsite, where water tumbles off old waste dumps. Nearby are two crumbling wooden structures and, as you turn toward the upper site, five more miners' shacks.

You will come to a good place to park next to wooden fences, marked with "no trespassing" signs, that protect a roofless log building that has served as a mine office and company store. Across the way, protected by the same fencing, is an impressive two-story boardinghouse built in 1939. To the west is an astonishing view of Lizard Head Peak, Wilson Peak, and Sunshine Mountain.

Also behind the fence, beyond the office and store, are four residences that housed mining officials. One of those houses has new siding on it and looks quite habitable, a change from my earlier visits. One home, probably

Framed by the middle window of the Alta company store and mine office is one of southwestern Colorado's most recognizable landmarks: Lizard Head Peak.

The weathered miners' dormitory at Alta once had an outside stairway to the second floor. Only its tilting roof remains.

the mining superintendent's, has an attractive bay window that likely has a spectacular view.

From the waste dump, you'll see lots of mining debris: buckets, pipe, slabs of concrete, and a geared wheel. Northeast of the boardinghouse are six wooden foundations and a log cabin. The schoolhouse once stood in this area, according to the 1955 topographic map.

WHEN YOU GO

From Telluride, head west to Colorado Highway 145. Turn south and drive 5.2 miles to the turnoff marked for Alta Lakes. The townsite comes into view in 3.5 miles. (The lakes are 1 mile beyond the Alta townsite.)

4

WYOMING

FOLLOWING THE

GHOST TRAILS

THE WORD "WYOMING" COMES FROM A DAKOTA WORD MEANING "LARGE PLAINS." A state couldn't be more aptly named. This chapter follows a route taken by more than three hundred thousand emigrants as they traversed the Wyoming Territory on the Oregon Trail, which extended two thousand miles from the Missouri River to Oregon City, Oregon. Southern branches of that trail led Mormons to their Zion and argonauts to their gold-filled California dreams. Later, the Oregon Trail became the course for the transcontinental telegraph and, for the westernmost Wyoming portion of the trail, the path of the Transcontinental Railroad—the means of transportation that made all the trails and routes obsolete.

Your journey begins thirty miles west of the Nebraska border at Fort Laramie, where the U.S. Army once protected trail pioneers. Nearby, at Guernsey, you can see signatures of those travelers and stand in the wheel ruts made by their wagons. Near South Pass City, the best ghost town in Wyoming, you cross South Pass, used by the pioneers because it was the gentlest ascent over the great mountains of the West. Then you visit Fort Bridger, another important way station along the Oregon Trail, where Mormon pioneers left the trail and headed to their destination, the Valley of the Great Salt Lake. A final stop west of Fort Bridger shows you a place that originally was a railroad camp for the Transcontinental Railroad.

A miner's cabin hides among the turning aspens at Miner's Delight, a tiny community that likely never reached a population of one hundred citizens.

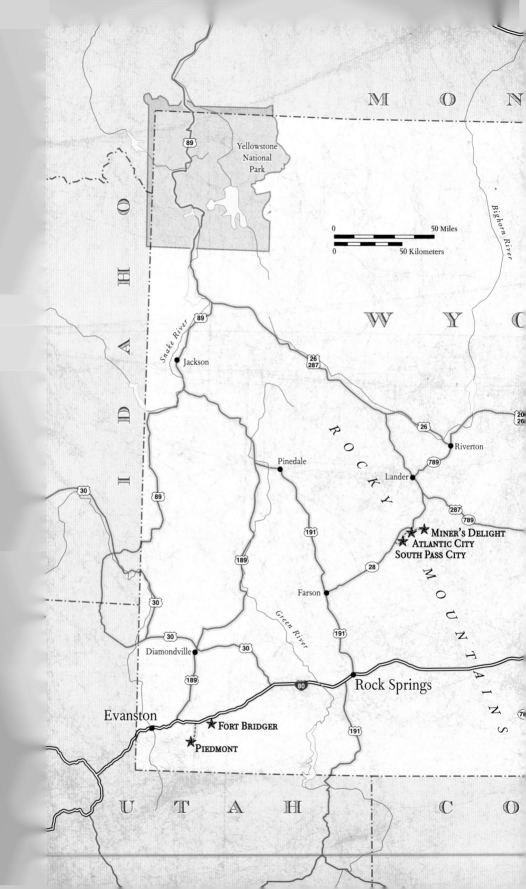

FORT LARAMIE

In 1834, fur trader William Sublette built a wooden stockade, called Fort William, near the confluence of the Laramie and Platte rivers to serve as a trading post with the Sioux and Cheyenne, who traded buffalo robes for such items as tobacco, beads, blankets, and munitions. The Platte ("flat" in French) was so named because it is wide but not deep, while the Laramie was named in honor of pioneer French trapper Jacques La Ramie, who had come to the area in about 1815 and died, likely at the hands of Indians, in about 1820.

Fort William was purchased by the American Fur Company two years later and rebuilt in 1841 into an adobe enclave officially known as Fort John. But to virtually anyone who traded there, it was commonly known as Fort Laramie.

Also in 1841, the U.S. Congress passed the Pre-emption Act, which had an enormous effect upon the Territory of Wyoming and Fort Laramie. Within two years, a westward movement of farmers seeking to claim public land, known as the Great Migration, began. For almost twenty years, the business at outposts like Fort Laramie became less about fur trading with Indians and much more about supplying goods to the more than three hundred thousand emigrants traversing the Oregon Trail.

In 1849, the U.S. Army purchased Fort Laramie because emigrants had begun to demand protection from Indians who were becoming increasingly hostile about the incursions into their traditional lands. A new post was erected, and Fort Laramie became a welcome sight on the Wyoming plains for the settlers who depended upon it, after one-third of their intended journey, for both supplies and

protection. During the peak years of the early 1850s, more than fifty thousand emigrants passed by Fort Laramie in the short summer season that lasted only about forty-five days. At that time, wagon train camps surrounded the fort as the pioneers purchased food and healthy draft animals while their equipment was serviced or repaired.

During the Civil War, the fort became a stop on the overland mail route and, later, the short-lived Pony Express. When the transcontinental telegraph was extended across Wyoming, Fort Laramie was an important station.

Fort Laramie declined in relevance as emigrant numbers dwindled in the 1860s. When the Transcontinental Railroad was completed in 1869, the Oregon Trail largely became a historical curiosity. Fort Laramie was abandoned in 1890 and its buildings auctioned off.

The 1874 cavalry barracks is the earliest building made of lime and concrete to survive in its entirety at Fort Laramie.

WALKING AROUND FORT LARAMIE

Many buildings still stand at the fort today because some were purchased and lived in by settlers while others were protected by concerned agencies as important to chronicling the story of the West.

From the parking area, it's a short distance to the tree-lined parade ground and a remarkable piece of American history. Start your tour at the 1884 Commissary Storehouse, now a visitors' center and museum.

Much of the fort is mere foundations, but many restored buildings have survived. Some of the best include the 1874 Cavalry Barracks, the largest structure at the fort; the 1875 Post Surgeon's Quarters and the 1884 Lieutenant Colonel's Quarters, both open for inspection and filled with period furnishings; and Old Bedlam, the oldest military building in Wyoming, having been erected in 1849. The lovely, two-story wooden barracks was in a ramshackle state until it was restored, a process that took from 1938 until 1964. Old Bedlam was the quarters of bachelor officers and was the site of much social merriment, likely accounting for the building's nickname.

The 1849 single officers' quarters was the center of social life at Fort Laramie, which likely accounts for its unofficial name, Old Bedlam.

The Lieutenant Colonel's Quarters (right), built in 1884, and the 1875 Post Surgeon's Quarters (behind) have been refurbished to look as they did in the 1880s.

WHEN YOU GO

The community of Fort Laramie is 106 miles northeast of Cheyenne via U.S. Highways 85 and 26. Historic Fort Laramie is 3 miles southwest of town. En route to the fort you will pass an 1875 military bridge that crosses the Platte River, a marker for the site of the short-lived trading post Fort Platte, and the Fort Laramie Cemetery.

Important note: After you leave Fort Laramie, travel 12 miles northwest on U.S. 85 and 26 to Guernsey to see the Oregon Trail Ruts State Historic Site and the Register Cliff State Historic Site. Both are located south of Guernsey on South Wyoming Avenue. At the former, you can stand in wheel ruts made by pioneer wagons; at the latter, you can read hundreds of signatures of emigrants who carved their names into the soft sandstone walls adjacent to the trail.

SOUTH PASS CITY

The Oregon Trail traversed the Continental Divide at South Pass, Wyoming, because it was a gentle ascent and descent over what was known as "Uncle Sam's Backbone." After the 1848 discovery of gold in California, hundreds of thousands of the trail pioneers headed over South Pass with dreams of getting in on the stories of incredible riches. They did not realize that they were practically tromping on a field of gold as they passed.

Although modest quantities of gold were discovered near South Pass as early as 1842, it wasn't until 1867 that a group of Mormon prospectors (or Fort Bridger soldiers—sources disagree) found what would become the Carissa Mine. Others rushed to the area and founded South Pass City near the site of an 1850s stagecoach stop and telegraph station. Founded at about the same time were two other smaller communities, Atlantic City and Miner's Delight. As many as three thousand citizens packed the three towns and the surrounding hills searching for gold—or in support, in one way or another, of those who were.

By 1868, the arrival of families had made South Pass City, despite its early rowdy reputation, a fairly civilized place. The men, women, and children of South Pass City enjoyed a main thoroughfare of hotels, general stores, butcher shops, a billiard parlor, a bowling alley, a school, and the usual saloons.

When I revisited South Pass City in 2007, it was a dusty, windy, and chilly September day. This and the other three photos of the townsite were taken in more peaceful conditions in August 2000. All buildings look much the same. This view taken of the community shows the Carissa Mine in the background.

WYOMING

South Pass City became the seat of Carter County in Dakota Territory, and, when Wyoming Territory was separated from Dakota Territory in 1869, it retained its county seat.

The big rush was remarkably short. The federal census of 1870 tallied 1,166 people in the entire mining district. By 1872, only a few hundred diehards held

South Pass City's Carissa Saloon served thirsty patrons sporadically until 1949. Behind it is the cabin in which Barney Tibbals, manager of the Carissa Mine, lived.

on. Subsequent explorations in the 1880s and 1890s brought some people back, followed by another small boom in the 1930s, as the Great Depression forced hundreds of former prospectors and miners to rework, in desperation, older diggings across the American West.

WALKING AROUND SOUTH PASS CITY

On your way to the townsite, you'll pass the enormous workings of the Carissa Mine, the principal reason for the existence of South Pass City, which closed for a final time in the 1950s. The State of Wyoming purchased the mine property in 2003 and intends to complete an interpretive center and offer a tour of the mill.

Most of the buildings at the Carissa, which produced somewhere between 60,000 and 180,000 ounces of gold, date from the 1930s.

South Pass City State Historic Site, just down the road from the Carissa, is now a quiet village that once pulsed with a much more vibrant heartbeat. At the visitors' center, located in an 1890s dance hall, you will receive an informative brochure that takes you through the almost three dozen standing buildings and ruins of South Pass City. The town is a classic example of a place whose structures were built of crude logs and hand-adzed beams on three sides, but with more genteel (and expensive) sawed boards as a false front. Of particular interest are the 1890s Carissa Saloon, the 1868 South Pass Hotel, an 1870s mercantile (now housing a gold mining exhibit with some life-size dioramas), and the 1890s schoolhouse. The school last served students in 1948. West of the schoolhouse is the Wolverine Mine, which features a ten-stamp mill.

Up the hill from the parking lot .3 of a mile is the South Pass City Cemetery, which consists of two headstones, two wrought-iron fences, and, very likely, many unmarked graves.

The Smith-Sherlock Company Store was built in 1896 using logs salvaged from the 1870 Episcopal church. The Sherlock family operated the general mercantile until 1948.

In the foreground stands the Exchange Saloon and Card Room. Next door is a restaurant erected by Janet Sherlock Smith in 1899 to support her South Pass Hotel, which is next door to the restaurant.

WHEN YOU GO

Start in Lander, about 255 miles west-northwest of Fort Laramie.

South Pass City, Atlantic City, and Miner's Delight are south of Lander. From Lander, head southeast for 8 miles on U.S. Highway 287 to the intersection with Wyoming Highway 28. The turnoff to the South Pass City area is clearly marked near milepost 43, about 29 miles from that intersection.

ATLANTIC CITY

Atlantic City was founded during the same mining boom that created South Pass City. It became a solid community with the usual businesses and services, including one truly sophisticated touch: a cigar store.

Like its neighbor, Atlantic City was mostly dead by the 1870s, but a resurgence took place in 1884 when French mining engineer Emile Granier attempted to use hydraulic mining to tap the riches of Rock Creek. After an investment of $250,000, the project failed in 1902.

St. Andrew's Episcopal Church is one of two excellent buildings in Atlantic City. This photo was taken in August 2000. The major change since then is that the church now has a ramp for handicapped access.

In 1960, United States Steel opened the Atlantic City Iron Ore Mine, which gave a modest rebirth to the community that accounts for several modern structures in town. That mine ceased production in 1983.

WALKING AND DRIVING AROUND ATLANTIC CITY

You might be a little disappointed when you enter town on Atlantic City Road. It lacks the charm of South Pass City because of many modern elements amid the historic structures—and a certain amount of clutter. The best building in

town, and the center of activity, is the Atlantic City Mercantile, built in 1893 by German immigrant Lawrence Giessler of adobe brick with a pressed-tin false front. Within its current incarnation as a steakhouse and bar, you can examine the mercantile's historic interior, complete with old photographs, various articles of antiquity, and a small museum. Also available is a self-guided Atlantic City tour pamphlet.

Another fine building is the 1913 St. Andrew's Episcopal Church, which was carefully restored between 1965 and 1967. Inside is attractive wainscoting matching the wooden ceiling. Both the church and the mercantile are on the National Register of Historic Places.

A tiny private cemetery sits just west of Dexter Street on the west side of town. The public cemetery is east of town up on the hill as Atlantic City Road turns northeast toward Miner's Delight.

WHEN YOU GO

To reach Atlantic City from South Pass City, retrace your route past the Carissa Mine for .6 of a mile and turn right. Atlantic City is 3.7 miles down that road.

MINER'S DELIGHT

Miner's Delight is one of the least known, most overlooked, and most rewarding ghost towns in this book. It is an unexpected delight.

A camp called Hamilton City began with the discovery of the Miner's Delight Mine in 1867. When that mine produced a modest bonanza of at least sixty thousand dollars in gold within two years, the camp appropriated the name of the mine. (A note about the apostrophe: The name probably should be "Miners' Delight," as it was meant to convey "the delight of miners." The topographic map eliminates the apostrophe altogether, which implies the U.S. Postal Service did the same thing much earlier. I am choosing "Miner's" because that is the way it most commonly turns up in historic documents and current accounts.)

One of the wonderful rewards to taking the walk down the path to Miner's Delight is seeing an abandoned community with something elusive: absolute solitude.

Many of the Miner's Delight cabins appear unstable, but they are propped up from within.

Miner's Delight's population likely never reached a hundred, peaking before 1882. The camp was deserted and in ruins in 1907, when speculators attempted to reopen the Miner's Delight Mine. The attempt was futile; a 1914 geologist's report noted that the mine was abandoned and flooded. During the Depression, several cabins were occupied, as in South Pass City and Atlantic City, by unemployed miners hoping to eke out a living.

WALKING AROUND MINER'S DELIGHT

You park your car adjacent to the tiny Miner's Delight Cemetery, with its solitary marker and three wrought-iron fences, and take a five-minute walk down a well-marked trail to see a true, abandoned ghost town listed on the National Register of Historic Places. Eight log cabins, propped up from within and held in a state of arrested decay, are protected by the Bureau of Land Management. Nearby are the remains of a small stamp mill.

The townsite sits amid a grove of aspens, which adds to the charm and solitude of this small treasure.

WHEN YOU GO

Head east and then north for 2 miles on the main road leading out of Atlantic City. Turn right and proceed for 2.8 miles to a sign directing you to the parking area for Miner's Delight.

Encampment

Encampment lies off the logical route that links the sites in this chapter, but I heartily recommend a side trip.

Early trappers called their summer rendezvous and trading spot with local Indians "Camp Le Grande." Later, the name was Anglicized to Grand Encampment and finally shortened to Encampment. The town, established in 1898, primarily served the Rudefeha Copper Mine (named after founding partners Rumsey, Deal, Ferris, and Haggarty). A sixteen-mile aerial tramway, completed in 1902, took copper ore, loaded into 985 buckets, from the Sierra Madre to a smelter in Riverside, adjacent to Encampment. Once a town of about two thousand, Encampment faded when a fire at the smelter closed operations in 1906, followed by a nationwide fall in the price of copper.

Today the town features one of Wyoming's best museums, the Grand Encampment Museum, which comprises fourteen historic buildings, each containing numerous unusual artifacts.

Outside the museum is a rare sight: a series of truncated towers of that Rudefeha tramway. The museum buildings include, among others, a farmhouse, a livery barn, the Palace Bakery and Ice Cream Parlor, the Kuntzman Building with its pressed tin façade, and a fire lookout station towering above the grounds. Inside the interpretive center, look for the unusual Mosely folding bathtub.

Encampment's business district features the 1904 two-story, brick E & H (for owners Emerson and Henry) Building, a 1902 opera house and town hall, and a handsome stone residence on the northeast corner of Sixth and Winchell streets that was intended to be a brothel. Citizens "invited" the prospective inhabitants to leave town before the structure was completed. It eventually served a more noble purpose as a boardinghouse for teachers.

The picturesque, well-tended Encampment Cemetery is northwest of town on Fourth Street. On one of my visits, deer were keeping the grass nicely trimmed.

Opposite: The Palace Bakery and Ice Cream Parlor was owned by the Koffman family in about 1900. Upstairs at one point was the Royal Neighbors of America Lodge. The Kuntzman Building was built by George Kuntzman in 1900 for his insurance office.

WHEN YOU GO

Encampment is 57 miles southeast of Rawlins. From Rawlins, take Interstate 80 east to Walcott, Exit 235. Encampment is 42 miles south of that exit on Wyoming Highways 130 and 230.

On your way south, you'll pass through Saratoga, which features a delightful downtown anchored by the marvelous 1893 Wolf Hotel. The Wolf offers accommodations and gourmet meals that attract diners from miles around.

The Grand Encampment Museum stands on Barrett Street in Encampment. When the highway into town turns right and becomes Sixth Street, turn left on Sixth instead and proceed east to Barrett.

FORT BRIDGER

Jim Bridger was an eighteen-year-old former blacksmith's apprentice when he came to the West in 1822, employed by the Rocky Mountain Fur Company as an explorer-trapper. In the next twenty years, he reached nearly mythical status as the West's preeminent guide.

In 1843, Bridger went into a kind of retirement and began a less well-known career as a businessman. He and his partner, Louis Vasquez, established Fort Bridger as a rendezvous point for trappers as early as 1825. Less a "fort" and more a trading post and blacksmith's shop, Fort Bridger served as a supply station for emigrant trains. More than three hundred thousand people—going to Oregon for farming opportunities, to the Valley of the Great Salt Lake for religious freedom, and to California for the prospect of great riches—passed along the route that included Fort Bridger after they had crossed the Continental Divide at South Pass (see South Pass City entry, pages 120–125).

The Latter-day Saints purchased the fort in 1855 as a dependable way station for Mormon pioneers headed to the Salt Lake Valley. The Mormons burned their fort in 1857 after a conflict with the U.S. Army, which in turn built a military outpost on the spot. That installation served off and on until it was abandoned in 1890, the same year Fort Laramie ceased operation.

WALKING AROUND FORT BRIDGER

An 1880s barracks now serves as a visitors' center and museum. As you head toward the barracks, you'll pass a cluster of outbuildings that include, among others, the post trader's store, a warehouse, a mess hall, the Pony Express barn, and the grave of Thornburgh, a dog whose feats of heroism are recounted on a sign adjacent to his grave.

The fort's combination visitors' center and museum features hundreds of artifacts, including a impressive cannon that was transported by mules and an informative timeline that traces the history of the fort. You will also be given a walking-tour brochure.

Jim Bridger's original fort stood near where that museum now stands, but a 1980s replica has been built a short distance to the northwest. It looks small and almost flimsy, but the original fort served its purpose and was a welcome sight to

This 1980s reconstruction of Jim Bridger's trading post stands northwest of the fort's original location.

The reconstruction of the trader's quarters at Fort Bridger features, in addition to a bed and a fireplace, a rifle and a collection of Native American items, including grinding stones.

This Victorian officers' quarters is filled with period furniture and memorabilia.

travelers. A red flag flies above the fort, a well-known indication to pioneers of a trading post. The post offers small items for sale, and a separate building within the stockade shows the trader's living quarters.

The most elegant buildings stand near the southeast boundary of the fort. One is the spacious, two-story clapboard Commanding Officer's Quarters, built in 1884. The other is identified in the brochure only as a "ranch house," but it was originally an officer's quarters also dating from the 1880s. Although it is smaller than the commanding officer's house (naturally), it is actually much more architecturally attractive. The two-story Victorian was sold at auction after the closing of the fort and moved off the property, serving nearby as a ranch house. It was returned in the 1970s and restored.

The Commanding Officer's Quarters has finely detailed window trim and an equally elaborate front porch.

WHEN YOU GO

From South Pass City, Atlantic City, and Miner's Delight, take Wyoming Highway 26 southwest 42 miles to Farson. From there, head 41 miles south on U.S. Highway 191 to Rock Springs and then 70 miles west on Interstate 80 to the town of Fort Bridger.

PIEDMONT

The westernmost and final site on your route along the historic trails across Wyoming is the ghost town of Piedmont. Although it's a small town that can only be viewed from a road, not truly explored, I enjoyed Piedmont enormously.

One reason I like Piedmont is its bee-hive charcoal kilns, which you will come upon just before you arrive at the townsite. I confess to being almost a kiln addict, having visited hundreds in the West, from New Mexico to California to Washington to Montana. Piedmont has three standing kilns and a fourth in ruins. Pioneer settler Moses Byrne built them in 1889 to provide fuel for smelters in the Utah Valley. The kilns are thirty feet high and thirty feet in diameter, a typical size for beehive kilns.

Kilns were crucial to the mining process. Smelting, which eliminates the impurities still in ore after the milling process, requires enormous heat. The materials available in the late 1800s for that heat were wood and coal, both of which burn too quickly and produce too little heat to be efficient. Kilns were used to convert a fast-burning, low-heat substance into a slow-burning, high-heat fuel. Wood was turned to charcoal; coal became coke. Think of your pre-propane backyard grill. Wood will not efficiently cook your burgers, but charcoal will.

These kilns are the first ones featured in this book, followed by ones at Nicholia and Bayhorse, Idaho; Frisco, Utah; and Ward, Nevada. They all converted wood to charcoal by heating wood in a controlled-burn process. Wood

You can view the Piedmont kilns without trespassing. This view, the side away from the road, shows the lower "front" doors to the kilns.

was loaded into a ground-level opening (the holes facing away from the road at Piedmont). First dry wood, followed by green wood, was stacked as high as possible. A higher door in the rear of the kiln (the side facing the road at Piedmont), which was reached through a ramp, was used to finish filling the kiln. Kilns of this size could hold up to fifty cords of wood. The doors were closed and sealed, the wood set afire, and the air within the kiln carefully regulated through vents that were alternately opened and sealed.

This slow "cooking" process would take about ten days. At that time, the kilns were opened and the fire was doused with water. The charcoal was removed and, after cooling, shipped to a smelter.

The process was very similar when coal was converted to coke. Such kilns, when using coal, are called "coke ovens."

The town of Piedmont, located immediately beyond the kilns, was initially called Byrne for Moses Byrne and his family. In 1868, when the Union Pacific Railroad came right through the Byrne property (you were driving on the original railroad bed as you came in), Byrne was renamed Piedmont (French for "at the foot of the mountains"). It became a tent town for the railroad construction crews and the eventual location of a roundhouse and water tank.

Piedmont remained an important spot on the Union Pacific until the railroad put a tunnel through Aspen Mountain, shortening the route and eliminating Piedmont entirely. Not surprisingly, the town became a ghost. The final resident was sheepherder William Taylor, who in 1949 froze to death in a blizzard.

WALKING AND DRIVING AROUND PIEDMONT

As mentioned earlier, you cannot explore the buildings of Piedmont, because they are on private property and posted against trespassing. But you can get a good view from the road of its dozen wooden buildings, seven of which are under roof at this writing. Binoculars or a telephoto lens on your camera will help you enjoy the site. Outside the "no trespassing" area are the aforementioned kilns and, south of the kilns, the Byrne family cemetery.

To reach the cemetery, I walked about 130 yards south from the road. (You have to hop over or step into a narrow manmade water-filled ditch.) More than two dozen gravestones mark the site, with every one identifying either a Byrne by birth or by marriage. A sign dates the cemetery from 1870 until 1931, but there are more recent graves than that. Patriarch Moses Byrne (1820 to 1904), who built the kilns, and his wife, Catherine (1829 to 1902), had at least five children. Of the ones buried in the Byrne Cemetery, Moses and Catherine outlived them all. One hopes there were other Byrne children not buried there.

Piedmont's remnants are what dedicated ghost town seekers yearn for. Just keep to the road to avoid trespassing.

WHEN YOU GO

From Fort Bridger, return to Interstate 80 and head west to Exit 24, Leroy Road, which is 10.3 miles from Fort Bridger. Take County Road 173 for 6.9 miles to the charcoal kilns. The Piedmont townsite is .2 of a mile beyond.

At 3.4 miles from the interstate, before you reach Piedmont, a plaque commemorates an important historic spot in southwestern Wyoming. A short distance away is the site of Muddy Creek Camp, where Brigham Young and the first group of Mormons, 149 in all, camped on their way to the Salt Lake Valley in July 1847. With plenty of water and grass, the camp became a principal stop for more than seventy thousand Mormons who followed. Later, the site became a resting point for the U.S. Army, the Pony Express, and a stagecoach line, the last of which built a station there. The coming of the railroad made Muddy Creek Camp unnecessary.

5

IDAHO

G H O S T S   O F   T H E
GEM STATE

THE GHOST TOWNS OF IDAHO BEGIN LESS THAN 175 MILES NORTHWEST OF PIEDMONT, Wyoming, the last site featured in chapter 4 (see pages 136–139). In fact, the first site featured in this chapter, Chesterfield, is the last place mentioned in this book that was a part of the Oregon Trail, which we followed throughout chapter 4.

This chapter will take you to ten ghost towns, all but the first related to mining. Gold was originally discovered in 1862 near what became Idaho City, and gold fever spread throughout the Idaho Territory, although it was later strikes of silver that made Idaho's fortune. Incidentally, the nickname the Gem State initially had nothing to do with minerals or precious stones: "Idaho" was a made-up word coined by those who for political reasons wanted an Idaho Territory proclaimed by Congress. They claimed *idaho* was an Indian word meaning "gem of the mountains." The name stuck, the nickname survived, and only much later did mineral wealth make the nickname a fact.

Note: Two sites in Idaho's Panhandle, Wallace and Burke, are not included in this chapter but rather in chapter 6 (see pages 216–225), on Montana ghost towns, because they are much closer in distance to the last site in that state than to the others in Idaho.

The Empire Saloon now serves as the visitors' center and park headquarters at Custer. Eventually, the building will be restored as a historic saloon.

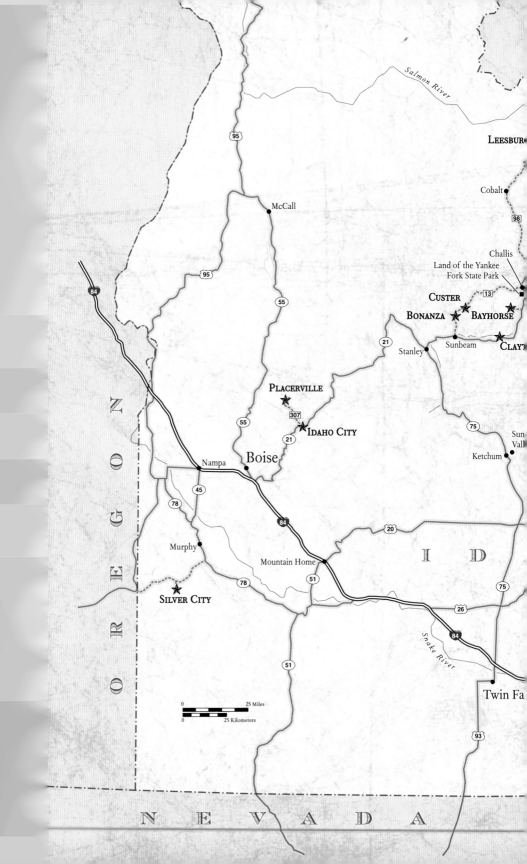

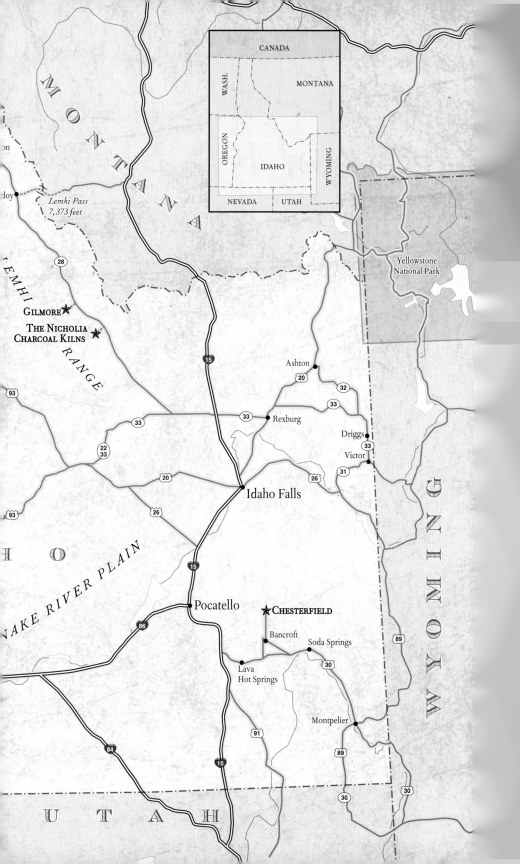

CANADA

WASH.

MONTANA

OREGON

IDAHO

WYOMING

NEVADA   UTAH

M O N T A N A

Lemhi Pass
7,373 feet

doy

on

LEMHI RANGE

28

GILMORE★

THE NICHOLIA
CHARCOAL KILNS ★

15

93

33

22
33

93

20

26

Ashton

20

32

33

33   Rexburg

Driggs

Victor

33

31

26

Idaho Falls

Yellowstone
National Park

W Y O M I N G

15

I D A H O

SNAKE RIVER PLAIN

86

Pocatello

★ CHESTERFIELD

Bancroft

Soda Springs

30

Lava
Hot Springs

89

84

91

Montpelier

89

15

30

30

U T A H

CHESTERFIELD

In 1879, Mormons Chester Call and his nephew, Christian Nelson, came to southern Idaho with three hundred grazing horses because land in northern Utah was becoming scarce. They were joined by other members of the Church of Jesus Christ of Latter-day Saints, and within two years the community of Chesterfield (named either for cofounder Chester Call or because it reminded a Mormon official of Chesterfield, England) was thriving, eventually reaching a population of more than four hundred. The selection of property lots was originally by lottery. In addition to agriculture, the town served as a supply point along the Oregon Trail, which was still in limited use in the 1870s.

The town's prosperity lasted for only a couple of generations. For one thing, the site was isolated, with a railroad and major roads bypassing it, making the winters difficult. For another, large-scale farming techniques doomed

Originally built by Nathan Barlow and Judson Tolman in about 1903, Chesterfield's Holbrook Mercantile closed in 1956 with Chester Holbrook as owner.

hundreds of rural communities across America by the end of World War II, and Chesterfield was one of them. The town's last business, the Holbrook Mercantile, somehow hung on until 1956. But unlike many villages that simply disappeared as huge farming conglomerates engulfed them, Chesterfield has survived.

WALKING AND DRIVING AROUND CHESTERFIELD

Chesterfield today contains almost two dozen historic buildings, fifteen of which are being or have been restored. Farm fields extend both north and south from the town boundaries.

The meeting house in Chesterfield was constructed between 1887 and 1892 of local brick crafted by hand.

As you enter the community, listed since 1980 on the National Register of Historic Places, you'll see several austere brick or log residences and the brick Call-Higginson-Muir Store (the bricks of Chesterfield were crafted locally). Another building of note is that last business in town, the brick Holbrook Mercantile, built about 1903 (and featuring two old gas pumps of different eras). On the northern fringe, as you head out of town down a short hill, stand two deserted log cabins and outbuildings.

But there's much more: The 1892 Meeting House (or church), now a museum, stands on a hill on the west edge of town, where you can obtain a brochure for further explorations. Next door is a 2003 reconstruction of the 1895 Amusement Hall, a community center. A roofless brick shell east of the hall is the remains of the 1922 schoolhouse, which burned in 2000 after being struck by lightning. South of the Meeting House .7 of a mile is the town's well-tended cemetery, still in use, which includes the graves of many founding families of Chesterfield.

The Tolman-Loveland home in Chesterfield, like the meetinghouse, was constructed of homemade brick. Note the second-story wooden balcony.

East of the Meeting House area is a second group of homes, including a few that are often open for visitation with volunteer docents. One pleasant residence is the Tolman-Loveland house, built by Bishop Judson A. Tolman in 1896 and purchased by Bishop Carlos Loveland in 1898. A small, wooden balcony projects from the second story. Across the street stands the tiny, two-room, brick tithing office, where financial matters of church members were settled.

One place easily overlooked is the Higginson-Holbrook property, because all that is visible of it from most of town is its windmill. When you take a dirt road that climbs a hill and passes in front of that windmill, you'll see a seven-gabled, two-story home, built about 1903. The rest of the buildings in Chesterfield are sturdy and solid—but staid. This alone has a stylish grace. One wonders if any Chesterfield residents considered it a bit "showy."

WHEN YOU GO

Evanston, Wyoming, is west of Piedmont, the last entry in the previous chapter (see pages 136–139). From Evanston, drive 93 miles northwest to Montpelier, Idaho, via Wyoming Highway 89 (which becomes Utah Highway 16 in Utah) north to Utah Highway 30 and then northwest to U.S. Highway 89, which goes north and then east into Montpelier. From Montpelier, take U.S. Highway 30 northwest for 29 miles to Soda Springs. Stay on U.S. 30 for 7 miles beyond Soda Springs until you come to a junction with Idaho Highway 30. Turn northwest on Idaho Highway 30 and go to Bancroft, a distance of 10 miles. From Bancroft, cross the railroad tracks and drive north 9.4 miles on Chesterfield Road to Chesterfield.

THE NICHOLIA CHARCOAL KILNS

The Nicholia Charcoal Kilns, sixteen in all, were erected in 1885 to provide fuel for the smelter at Nicholia, today a site of two log cabins within a private ranch. The smelter reduced the ore from the Viola, a lead and silver mine, which was located in a canyon above Nicholia. The mine began production in 1881 and yielded $2.5 million in paying ore. The same smelter also processed ore from Gilmore (see following entry, pages 150–151).

The Nicholia beehive brick kilns were used to convert wood to charcoal. An informative sign near the kilns describes the process. You can also find out more about how kilns work in the Piedmont, Wyoming, entry (pages 136–139).

Loggers decimated the Douglas fir forests of the Lemhi Range for wood for these kilns, located at the mouth of Coal Kiln Canyon (a misnomer: there was no coal, only wood). The sixteen kilns used about 75,000 cords of wood per year. No doubt you have seen huge logging trucks lumbering (sorry) down the highway. The interpretive sign says those trucks carry approximately ten cords per load; however, a forestry industry spokesman told me that a truck actually carries more like 6.25 cords per load. That would mean the kilns used 12,000 truckloads per year, or 33 per day for every single day of the year. As the kilns were in production for five years, you can imagine the effect upon the local forest.

When ore production ceased at the Nicholia smelter in 1890, the reason for the kilns to fire ceased as well. An astonishing forty acres of neatly stacked four-foot-long cordwood, ready for processing to charcoal, was left abandoned near the kilns. Most of the wood was carried off, as were the bricks of twelve of the kilns, for use by settlers in the Lemhi Valley, north of Gilmore, and in the Snake River Plain, to the southeast.

We may be able to see only four of Nicholia's sixteen original kilns, but they are a marvelous sight. Two are partial, the other two virtually complete. Each was originally twenty feet high, plastered almost a foot thick. Be sure to take the walking loop tour, as you will learn a great deal about the kilns and the surrounding area.

The Nicholia Charcoal Kilns sit in lovely Birch Creek Valley with the Lemhi Range as a backdrop.

WHEN YOU GO

From Chesterfield, drive to Idaho Falls, a distance of about 102 miles. From Idaho Falls, take Interstate 15 north for 24 miles to Idaho Highway 33. Turn left (west) and proceed 15 miles to the junction with Idaho Highway 28. Follow Highway 28 northwest for 47 miles to the turnoff to the charcoal kilns. A large interpretive sign stands across the street from the turnoff. The kilns themselves are 5.2 miles west of the sign.

GILMORE

Gilmore features the largest remnants of a silver and lead mining boom that began in the 1870s and ended in the 1920s in the Birch Creek Valley. Originally known as Horseshoe Gulch, the settlement began as a cluster of cabins near the early diggings in the late 1880s. A stagecoach line connected Horseshoe Gulch to the outside world, and in 1902, the town's citizens elected to change the community's name to honor Jack T. Gilmer, one of the owners of the stage company. The U.S. Postal Service approved the name but accidentally spelled it "Gilmore." Townspeople apparently decided to accept the error rather than fight the federal bureaucracy.

The town was moved down from what is still known as Horseshoe Gulch in 1910 to its present location when the Gilmore & Pittsburgh Railroad—a branch line beginning at Armstead, Montana (now submerged beneath Clark Canyon Reservoir, southwest of Dillon)—arrived in that year. The G&P Railroad was known derisively as the Get off and Push. With the arrival of the railroad, town honoree Jack Gilmer's stage line was obsolete.

Gilmore's Pittsburgh-Idaho group of mines (financial backing came principally from Pennsylvanians) continued into the late 1920s, second only in production to the Coeur d'Alene silver mines in northern Idaho (see the Wallace entry, pages 216–223). Gilmore's prosperity ended when a power plant explosion and resulting fire in 1927 ended large-scale mining after producing $11.5 million in silver and lead. The railroad ceased service, and the rails were sold for scrap in 1940. The post office somehow hung on, perhaps by federal indifference (after all, they got the name wrong in the first place), until 1957.

WALKING AND DRIVING AROUND GILMORE

As you head from the highway up into Gilmore, you will see the old roadbed from the G&P Railroad as you cross it. More than two dozen buildings, ranging from habitable to tumbledown, remain at the town.

At the main intersection in Gilmore, you will be facing the very long, one-story, wood-frame general mercantile, which is covered with ornamental tin. The false front has three messages, the top bleeding into the middle, as they were painted in different years: The top reads "U.S. Post Office." Halfway underneath

Gilmore's impressive general mercantile should look considerably better than this in the future: The Lemhi County Historical Society intends to restore the ravaged building.

is "Gilmore Mercantile," with "general merchandise" below that. Painted in large letters on the north side of the building's roof is the town's name. The store was built by the Ross brothers in 1910, the year the railroad came to Gilmore. (The building has been purchased by the Lemhi County Historic Preservation Committee and the Lemhi County Historical Society and Museum for preservation and restoration.)

In addition to several log cabins and wood-frame residences is a two-story wood building, now painted red, that served as the automobile repair shop. It stood adjacent to the rail line, where new autos shipped to the Birch Creek Valley could be unloaded and serviced on the spot. The second floor had living quarters.

Up the road beyond the townsite .4 of a mile are several deteriorating log cabins. A large log structure, which might have been the base of an ore hopper, is just beyond. This is Horseshoe Gulch, the original townsite.

Continue uphill on the road beyond the gulch. In .3 of a mile, an unmarked road, definitely not for passenger cars, takes a sharp turn up to the left. This leads in .1 of a mile to the town's cemetery, which contains several markers in two sections. The prominent grave, a recent addition, is for Dick Moll, who was the unofficial guardian, historian, and chief advocate for the preservation of Gilmore. Moll, called The Gilmore Kid on his marker, died in 2002.

WHEN YOU GO

From the turnoff to the Nicholia Charcoal Kilns, continue northwest on Idaho Highway 28 for 11.8 miles to the turnoff to Gilmore. The town is 1.5 miles west of that turnoff.

LEESBURG

Leesburg could serve as a model for what a deserted ghost town should be. You park your car next to a kiosk that features a series of highly informative signs that provide details of the townsite. Leesburg itself, with its approximately fifteen buildings, is a short walking-distance away. A tiny cemetery is a short walk from the town.

Preservationists of other such sites would do well to look at Leesburg. First, because of the parking area and the plaques, visitors know that this is not an abandoned site and that damaging anything would have severe consequences. Second, visitors learn an enormous amount from the signs, which one hopes would make people treat the site with the respect it deserves. And, finally, by putting this information away from the site instead of on signs in front of buildings, visitors, when walking into Leesburg, feel the desolation, the palpable sense of history, along with just enough eeriness to make people know they are in a special place.

Leesburg came to life in 1866 after Frank Sharkey and his party found placer gold in nearby creeks. Named by Confederate sympathizers for Robert E. Lee, Leesburg might have become just another quickly abandoned mining site with rich but shallow prospects. But in addition to placer gold, primary deposits were found in the hills, and hard-rock mining eventually brought three thousand gold-seekers to the town. Eventually, nearly a hundred businesses were established, including a newspaper. A competing town, named Grantsville by those who favored the Union side in the recently ended Civil War, developed east of Leesburg, but only the name Leesburg stuck. As primary deposits waned, hydraulic operations began in the presumably played-out placer deposits, and

Leesburg's main street features, from left, a butcher shop, a post office, a schoolhouse, and the tax assessor's office.

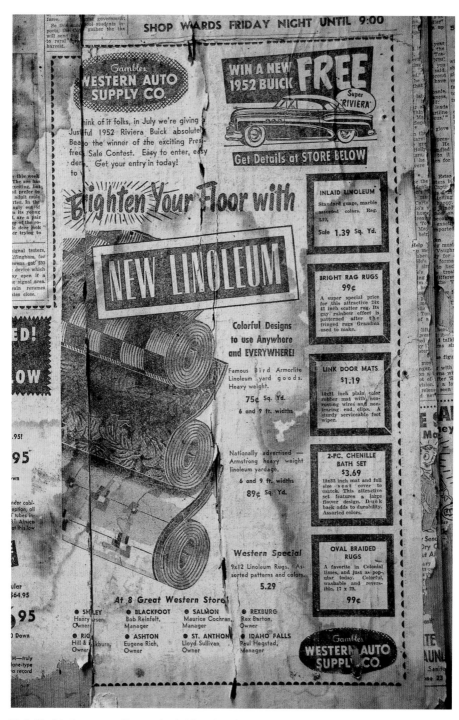
The inside of the former post office is insulated, if that's the right word, with newspapers from the 1950s.

IDAHO

new fortunes were made. Supplies came from newly opened routes from Boise through Idaho City to Salmon, where pack trains kept Leesburg alive, even requiring sleighs and dogsleds during the winter months. We think of stagecoaches as being relics that were retired in the late 1800s, but, amazingly, until a truck road was completed in the early 1930s, Leesburg was served by four or five stages and freighters daily, according to Salmon resident Jim Caples, who rode the stage each summer from 1926 until 1930.

Despite the road, Leesburg was moribund after World War II when the diggings finally gave out, but not before producing an estimated forty million dollars in gold.

WALKING AROUND LEESBURG

Those informative panels at the parking area give you detailed information on Leesburg, so I'll just give a brief summary: The site includes residences, an 1890s tax assessor's office, a 1935 schoolhouse, Mike and Maude Fraker's 1937 post office (which has old newspapers glued to the walls for insulation), a 1902 butcher shop, an 1890s Chinese laundry (Chinese made up almost half the population in 1880), the stagecoach office, an 1870s stable that later became a saloon, a boardinghouse, the Leesburg Hotel, and more. The hotel once had a very genteel feature: It offered a covered walkway to the other side of the street.

You passed the entrance to the cemetery on your way to town. From the parking lot, head back down the road .3 of a mile, where you will see on your right a walkover across a buckrail fence. Five headstones, a metal fence, and a couple of wooden fences make up the graveyard.

WHEN YOU GO

Leesburg is 31.6 miles northwest of Salmon. From Salmon, which is 61 miles northwest of the turnoff to Gilmore, head south on U.S. Highway 93 for 5.1 miles to Forest Service Road 021 and turn west. In 13.4 miles, you'll come to an intersection at a summit, but continue straight on FS Road 021. In another 2.8 miles, there's another intersection: FS Road 021 continues to Cobalt; Forest Service Road 098 goes right to Leesburg, now 10.3 miles away. The entire route is a wide, smooth road, because it is the haul road for the Beartrack Mine, which is adjacent to Leesburg. Ignore the turnoff to the Beartrack Mine .3 of a mile before the townsite. FS Road 098 dead-ends at the Leesburg parking area.

BAYHORSE

Bayhorse will look markedly different on your visit than it does in this book's photographs, and that will be good news. For decades, Bayhorse was privately owned and off-limits to visitors. The best one could do was to gaze and photograph from across Bayhorse Creek, trying to get a good look through the trees and brush.

The Idaho Department of Parks and Recreation, however, now owns the site, and in 2009 Bayhorse was opened to the public after an extensive clean-up of mine tailings, a slag dump, and even the town itself, which was poisoned with arsenic, among other dangerous materials. You cannot actually enter the buildings at this point because they are unsafe after, in some cases, more than a century of neglect. I was, nevertheless, given special permission to enter and photograph Bayhorse in 2007 after agreeing to obey several admonitions because of toxic, unsafe areas.

The most-repeated version of the naming of the mining district, the creek that runs through it, and the town that grew there is that a single prospector worked the area in about 1864 with the assistance of two bay horses. Other area prospectors couldn't remember his name, so he was identified as "the fellow with the bay horses."

Beginning in 1872, other prospectors working along Bay Horse Creek found promising silver deposits, but the real rush to the area didn't occur until Tim Cooper and Charley Blackburn discovered their Ramshorn claim in 1878. They sold it to others for a rather modest price because they lacked the capital to develop a mine in such a remote location.

As other deposits were discovered, the mining camp of Bayhorse (likely shortened to one word by the U.S. Postal Service) grew on a flat area along the north side of the creek. By 1882, a stamp mill and a smelter were built immediately west of town. Coke to fuel the smelter was initially shipped all the way from Pennsylvania, but the completion of six charcoal kilns on the south side of the creek later that same year created a less expensive local supply of fuel.

The State of Idaho's Department of Parks and Recreation is shoring up all the buildings at Bayhorse, including the enormous Bayhorse Mill.

In that same year, Bayhorse had about three hundred citizens and featured several saloons, boardinghouses, a meat market, and a general store. The peak years were the 1880s, but dropping silver prices, culminating in the Silver Crash of 1893, led to the town's decline, despite limited mining efforts between 1902 and 1918. The post office managed to hang on until 1927.

WALKING AND DRIVING AROUND BAYHORSE

Now that the Idaho Department of Parks and Recreation has completed its work on Bayhorse sufficiently to allow you to enter, you'll be parking atop the old smelter's slag dump, which has been capped because of hazardous materials beneath. You'll be able to see, on the west end of town, the huge Bayhorse Mill, built in 1882 by John Gilmore and O. J. Salisbury. The stamp mill was remodeled in 1919 to become a flotation mill and plant.

East of the mill is the 1880s stone Wells Fargo building with its heavy iron doors, followed by several cabins and outbuildings, and the two-story 1880s Bayhorse Hotel, the only hotel remaining of several that once stood in town. Across from the hotel are the collapsed remains of the so-called tin can building, a log, false-front, tin-covered structure that probably served as a livery stable and perhaps later as a garage.

Farther down the street is a two-story residence that was built as a one-story log structure in about 1883. A second story was added in the late 1880s to serve as the home of Charles and Agnes Baker. Mrs. Baker worked in the Bayhorse Hotel, which at that time was owned by her mother. Her husband had served as a medical orderly during the Civil War, and, although he was not a licensed physician, he used the skills he had learned in the war to practice medicine in Bayhorse and nearby mining camps.

The Baker House features an outdoor stairway to the second floor, indicating that it likely had boarders living above the family residence. Other wood, stone, and log remnants stand beyond the home.

On the south side of Bayhorse Creek are several other attractions, beginning with the six partially dismantled charcoal kilns (mislabeled on the topographic map as "coke ovens"), made of uncut stone and mortar. Beyond them are the ruins of a miner's log cabin.

West of the kilns .1 of a mile, up to the left along the road, is the tiny Bayhorse Cemetery with eight dilapidated wooden fences for individual graves. There are no markers. One has the feeling, walking around the graveyard, that there are many unmarked graves.

Immediately beyond the cemetery is a large log structure, possibly the base of an ore hopper. You can also see, on the opposite side of the canyon, considerable mining remnants of Bayhorse: The canyon walls are crisscrossed with mining trails and pockmarks of failed adits.

About three miles above town, on four-wheel-drive-only roads, are the remains of the Ramshorn and Skylark mines.

WHEN YOU GO

From Challis, which is 60 miles southwest of Salmon, drive southeast on U.S. Highway 93 to Idaho Highway 75, a distance of 2.3 miles. At that junction stands the Land of the Yankee Fork Interpretive Center, which features highly worthwhile exhibits and artifacts, along with knowledgeable personnel. From the interpretive center, turn south on Highway 75 and proceed 7.9 miles to Bayhorse Creek Road (Forest Service Road 051). You will cross the Salmon River by bridge and travel 3.2 miles to the site of Bayhorse.

The charcoal kilns at Bayhorse were built using mortar from the tailings pile of the Bayhorse Mill.

CLAYTON

Clayton is a minor ghost town that partially owes its existence to Bayhorse (see preceding entry, pages 156–159). The excitement on Bayhorse Creek, sixteen miles away, caused Joel E. Clayton to erect a smelter on the banks of the Salmon River in 1880. Even though his original smelter was of considerable size, the success of Bayhorse and other nearby mines led Clayton to double the size of his smelter in 1888. It finally closed down with the apparent depletion of the area's ore in 1902.

The closing was premature. Discoveries of new ore bodies, along with more efficient milling methods, led to a resurgence of area mining. By 1935, Clayton had become Idaho's greatest single producer of silver. A later discovery of scheelite (tungsten) brought further prosperity in the 1950s. In the 1980s, molybdenum deposits northwest of Clayton renewed area mining.

In Clayton today, a roadside sign provides historical information about the town. Walk behind the sign toward the riverbank to see the large slag pile of the old smelter. One block north stands the restored 1881 Idaho Mining and Smelter Company Store, now a museum open on summer weekends. The building also served as the post office from 1910 until 1921. The false front has "L. B. Worthington Dry Goods and Groceries" painted on it, reflecting new ownership in 1930. In 1933, it was sold again, and the large front windows of the store show that change: "Leuzinger General Merchandise."

A paved road on the west end of the mercantile, Forest Service Road 530, passes a sturdy brick schoolhouse, now a residence, and heads north from town, paralleling Kinnikinic Creek. It takes you in 1.6 miles to the considerable remains of the Clayton Mine, which operated into the 1980s, when a cave-in ended production. One mile east of town, on a hill north of the highway, stands the Clayton Cemetery.

WHEN YOU GO

From the junction of Bayhorse Road and Idaho Highway 75, drive southwest 13.2 miles to Clayton.

Claytons's Idaho Mining and Smelter Company Store has been beautifully restored and is open on summer weekends.
Even if it is closed, be certain to gaze through the large windows.

BONANZA, THE YANKEE FORK DREDGE, AND CUSTER

Placer gold deposits were discovered in 1870 by Sylvester Jordan and Captain Dudley B. Varney along a tributary of the Yankee Fork of the Salmon River. (Captain Varney is only the second person with my surname that I have found in my ghost town travels.) That small tributary, later known as Jordan Creek in Sylvester Jordan's honor, enticed a stream of prospectors to descend upon the remote diggings. Securing necessary supplies became an immediate problem. In 1876, the town of Challis was built as a center for the distribution of goods to the Yankee Fork mines. A toll road from Challis to the Yankee Fork area, completed in 1879, provided a link to the outside world.

BONANZA was the first mining camp along the Yankee Fork, founded in 1877 by Charles Franklin to serve the prospectors and miners who had rushed to the area. A town of more than six hundred people, the community had refinements not often found in placer mining camps: baseball and croquet fields, a watchmaker's shop, an actual street grid, and community wells with a piped water system for drinking and fire protection. That system, however, was not sufficient to protect Bonanza from major fires in 1889 and 1897. After the second conflagration, most people moved to neighboring Custer. When the final mine closed near Bonanza, the town was moribund.

WALKING AND DRIVING AROUND BONANZA

Bonanza today is a minor site with a few standing, leaning, and tumbling cabins. If you follow Forest Service Road 074 to the west, in one-half mile you'll arrive at the Bonanza Cemetery. This graveyard features an informative sign that relates how different ethnic groups contributed to the Idaho mining boom. Large numbers of Canadians, Germans, Englishmen, Irishmen, and Swedes worked the area. Cornish miners were employed by English bosses at the General Custer Mine. Austrians were imported for their road-building skills. Italians were preferred anywhere there were kilns, as they were experts at the controlled-heat process of turning wood to charcoal. The Chinese comprised the largest single group, reworking picked-over placer claims, running family-owned laundries, and

Bonanza's tumbling buildings sit right along the main road, which may partially account for why they are deteriorating so rapidly.

working as clerks in various businesses. There are, however, no graves of Chinese in this cemetery: Their remains were temporarily buried but then later disinterred for transportation back to China. Large organizations existed for this cultural service, especially during the California Gold Rush.

One of those buried in the cemetery is Captain Dudley Varney. He originally came to the West in 1864 with one of Jim Bridger's expeditions before making the claim on the Yankee Fork with partner Jordan.

Many replacement wooden markers, along with approximately a dozen headstones, are in the cemetery. One child's grave is marked with a "cradle" fence and an arch, from which flower baskets were suspended.

A second cemetery, Boot Hill, is .9 of a mile beyond the first. It contains only three graves and a sign telling of a grisly mystery: Realtor Richard King died in an argument with his business partner. His wife, Lizzie, and a friend, Charles Franklin, bought three burial plots. It was assumed they were for Richard and, eventually, the two of them. Lizzie, despite rumors of an impending wedding

The Yankee Fork Dredge is a rarity in the American West. Since it was not salvaged, it sits virtually intact in a pond of its own making.

to Franklin, married Bonanza newcomer Robert Hawthorne. The two subsequently were found dead. Charles Franklin left the area and was eventually found dead in his cabin clutching a locket containing a picture of Lizzie King. Was he a double murderer and then a suicide victim? Or were, perhaps, the newly married couple's deaths a murder-suicide? Whatever the answer, people in Bonanza did not wish to bury their loved ones near such tainted ground, and the graves of Richard King, Lizzie King, and Robert Hawthorne are the only ones at Boot Hill. The name of the cemetery, like many such notorious gravesites throughout the American West, comes from the expression "they died with their boots on," meaning violently. In this case, the term applies to all three people residing there.

THE YANKEE FORK DREDGE stands north of the townsite of Bonanza very near the spot of Varney and Jordan's original find at the confluence of Jordan Creek and the Yankee Fork.

The dredge was constructed about five miles downstream at Pole Flat in 1940. It worked its way north, creating its own standing pond in the Yankee Fork, chewing through the river bottom and upturning the bed into huge piles of river rock, which you drove through on your way to Bonanza. The dredge

operated until 1952, with a hiatus during World War II, when Law 208 made mining of non-war-related minerals illegal. First, the good news: The dredge recovered more than a million dollars' worth of gold and silver. Next, the bad news: It cost slightly more than it recovered to run the dredge. The huge operation, which lasted about eight years, was essentially a wash. But in its day, according to local author-historian Howard A. Packard Jr., it was quite a sight: "The Yankee Fork gold dredge looked like a well-lighted four-story hotel, lost in the mountains."

The schoolhouse at Custer would likely have disappeared were it not for Tuff and Edna McGown, who saved it and turned it into a museum in 1960.

A self-guided tour of the Yankee Fork Dredge is well worth the modest admission, and, because it is self-guided, you may take as little or as much time as you like. Parents with small children may appreciate that option.

CUSTER was founded in 1879, two years after Bonanza. The town was named for the area's principal mine, the General Custer, which had been discovered in 1876, not long after the famous Battle of Little Bighorn in that same year in which Custer made his last stand.

The town was founded by Samuel L. Holman, a graduate of Harvard Law School who headed to the West shortly after the death of his fiancée. He became the first justice of the peace in the recently created community of Bonanza, but he also worked claims along the Yankee Fork. As the General Custer Mine prospered, Holman saw that his claims would be more profitable as city lots, so in 1879, he laid out the town of Custer, which eventually surpassed Bonanza in importance. That occurred after a thirty-stamp mill was constructed north of town to process the estimated nine hundred tons of ore per month that were yielding about a million dollars' worth of gold annually.

The Yankee Fork's mineral wealth played out in the early years of the twentieth century, and both Bonanza and Custer eventually emptied. Only the Yankee Fork Dredge brought the area back to life beginning in 1940.

WALKING AND DRIVING AROUND CUSTER

Now a state park (donations are accepted, but there is no admission charge), Custer contains several buildings of interest, including one of the more photogenic false-front buildings in Idaho, the Empire Saloon. The structure was built sometime before 1903 and is now used as the park's headquarters. Across the street from the saloon is the 1900 former schoolhouse, now a very worthwhile museum. A walking tour brochure will increase your enjoyment of the town.

As you leave Custer heading north, on your right you'll see the stepped-down hillside marking the location of the General Custer Mine's mill, which, like several other buildings, burned in 1986 as the result of a fire caused by a carelessly discarded cigarette.

The Custer Cemetery is a mile north of town on the west side of the road. Seven marked graves are at the site, including one of antiquity. It is for Julian Riley Thompson, and his is a story of true pathos: As an infant, Julian suffered from convulsions, so his mother bathed the child in warm water to ease the symptoms. To be certain the water would always be ready, a kettleful was kept on the stove. On one fateful occasion, Julian's mother retrieved the kettle only to find it empty; a houseguest had used the water to wash dishes. The frantic mother rushed to a nearby saloon and returned with hot water, only to find that she was too late. Julian Thompson died in 1881 at seven months of age.

WHEN YOU GO

From Clayton, drive west on Idaho Highway 75 for 19.7 miles to Sunbeam. Turn north on Yankee Fork Road (Forest Service Road 013) and proceed 7.8 miles north to Bonanza. Where the road turns from pavement to dirt, you will see extensive evidence of the tailings of dredging operations extending north to Bonanza. In fact, you'll be driving on a smoothed portion of it.

IDAHO CITY

Idaho City has a look of permanence that most mining camps lack. Many buildings are made of brick, and, in fact, several views of the town could be mistaken for some of the better-preserved sites of the California Gold Rush. In addition to its permanence, the community also has enough life that it should be considered a historic town rather than a ghost town. Idaho City, however, is neither overly touristy nor overly dressed up: Parts are almost dowdy, which I find makes it all the more charming and photogenic.

In 1862, a party of men led by George Grimes and Moses Splawn discovered placer deposits in what later became known as Grimes Creek. The usual rush to the area ensued, and the Boise Basin came alive. The principal town was Idaho City, which had a population of about six thousand within a year. That made the boomtown the largest community in the Idaho Territory, and at one point it was reputed to be the largest city in the northwestern United States, bigger even than Portland, Oregon. But its size and prosperity was soon eclipsed by other strikes like Silver City and Montana's Virginia City and Helena. The raucous, bustling town of Idaho City began a decline within a few years as miners raced to the next El Dorado.

The town did not completely wither, however, as area mines continued to produce, albeit in less spectacular amounts. Later hydraulicking of hillsides and dredging of streambeds kept the Boise Basin producing for decades. The drive to Placerville (see following entry, pages 172–175) shows extensive evidence of this later mining.

WALKING AND DRIVING AROUND IDAHO CITY

A good place to start enjoying this architecturally diverse community is on Main Street, where you will find the 1865 Boise Basin Mercantile on the southwest corner of Main and Commercial streets. It lays claim to being Idaho's oldest store still in existence.

One block north, on the southwest corner of Main and Wall streets, stands the 1871 Boise County Courthouse. A single-story brick edifice that was originally built as a general store, it also served as a tin shop, a hardware store, and a hotel, finally becoming a courthouse in 1909. If it's open, be sure to observe its delightful interior, which looks, except for a few modernities, much as it did in 1909.

The Boise County Courthouse in Idaho City has served in that capacity for more than a century. Its courtroom, still in use, has been restored to its early-twentieth-century appearance.

North of the courthouse is the 1891 city hall, at Main and School streets, a two-story, wooden structure with an imposing bell tower. The building originally served as the town's school until 1962.

West of Main is Montgomery Street, which features other excellent buildings. On the northwest corner of Montgomery and Wall streets stands the Boise Basin Museum, housed in the 1867 former post office. West of the museum on Wall Street are the Idaho City Firehouse and the two-story, wood-frame Masonic Temple. Beyond the temple is the fourteen-cell, 1864 penitentiary, used by both Boise County and the Territory of Idaho. Made of huge hewn logs, it was moved to this location in 1952 and now has a protective roof.

On a hill east of town, on High Street, stand the 1867 St. Joseph Catholic Church and the 1875 Odd Fellows Hall.

Idaho City's Pioneer Cemetery (the topographic map identifies it as the Boot Hill Cemetery) is west of town on Centerville Road, which is on the north end of town. Go west on Centerville .3 of a mile, turn south on Buena Vista Road, and follow the road for .5 of a mile around to the right and up a hill.

The early morning sun touches Idaho City's city hall, erected as the town's schoolhouse in 1891. The building served students until 1962, when they moved to a new school on the north edge of town.

A sign at the cemetery states that an estimated three thousand people are buried there, but fewer than three hundred have been identified. Graves are spread over several acres in five separate sections, including the General (Public), Catholic, Masonic, Odd Fellows, and Chinese. The latter, as explained in the Bonanza entry (see page 162), contains no actual remains.

You could spend hours walking this pleasant, shady cemetery. One grave worth noticing is slightly uphill to the right beyond the sign showing the layout of the graveyard. A heavy, Gothic-looking, iron fence, with each panel showing a reclining lamb under a weeping willow, surrounds the more than eight-foot-long horizontal stone covering the grave of Mary E. Pinney, who died in 1869 at twenty-five years of age. The stone is engraved from top to bottom, and a wooden sign next to it helps you read the stone.

WHEN YOU GO

From Bonanza, return to Sunbeam. Drive west for 13 miles on Idaho Highway 75 to Stanley, one of the most spectacularly beautiful spots on this Earth. From Stanley, follow Idaho Highway 21 to Idaho City, a distance of 90 miles.

Idaho City's Masonic Lodge was built in 1865. It still contains original furnishings.

PLACERVILLE

As the name implies, Placerville in 1862 was the site of placer gold deposits. The town reportedly had a population of five thousand a year later and was incorporated in 1864. Placerville became the major supply point for the dozens of diggings attempted in hopeful emulation of the original strike. The community had saloons, butcher shops, a church, blacksmith shops, drugstores, hotels, and restaurants, but it also had signs of gentility: a millinery and a dressmaker's shop.

As the easy placering declined, hard-rock mining began, along with hydrau-licking of the hillsides above the original placer strikes. But by 1870, the town had shrunk to a population of only 318, many of whom were Chinese working the so-called played-out claims that other miners had given up on. The town partially burned several times, and a fire in 1899 nearly destroyed it. By that time, Placerville was already in decline, although much of the town was still rebuilt.

Evidence of the extensive placering is found today southwest of town along the Mud Flat tailings of Granite Creek and Fall Creek, and the topographic map shows three nearby placer mines: the Halley, the Reid, and the Leary.

WALKING AND DRIVING AROUND PLACERVILLE

Placerville is a delightful, well-groomed community covering one square mile and featuring many summer cabins, several of them of from its glory days. A large town square, known as the Plaza since pioneer days, is a pleasant site for gatherings, with roof-covered picnic tables and nearby restrooms. But the real stars of the town are a white, two-story Masonic Lodge, the 1865 Magnolia Saloon, the Boise Basin Mercantile Company, an Episcopal church just west of town, and a picturesque cemetery.

Both the saloon and the mercantile are now museums, open on summer weekends. Even if the museums are closed, they're well worth peering into. The Boise Basin Mercantile has original fixtures, counters, and old stock items. The Magnolia Saloon looks like a museum, not a saloon, but it still features one wall with original wallpaper dating from the saloon's heyday.

As the signs say, the Boise Basin Mercantile even carried gas, oil, and auto accessories. A side sign announces that the store also once sold Owyhee candy, made in Boise. For more on the word *Owyhee*, see the Silver City entry, page 176.

Placerville's Magnolia Saloon does not have the normal false front. Notice the creative way the lettering problem was solved, even when a window intrudes.

The turnoff to the Placerville Cemetery is .2 of a mile west of the town square, where you'll head south and proceed up to the entry gate.

The cemetery features such diverse groups as Masons, Catholics, and Odd Fellows, apparently well mixed together, unlike many graveyards that are completely sectioned off by affiliation. Several of the people buried there came from Scotland and Ireland.

Placerville is 13.5 miles northwest of Idaho City. Take Centerville Road (Forest Service Road 307), which leaves Idaho City on the north end of town, for 12.4 miles. At that point, Harris Creek Road joins FS Road 307. Turn north and proceed 1.1 miles to Placerville.

SILVER CITY

Not only is Silver City the ghost town gem of the Gem State, it is one of the very best in the West. The almost seventy buildings of Silver City are occupied and maintained, but they are not overly restored, so the town has a distinctly noncommercial look to it. Many of the structures are wonderful architectural examples of the 1870s. The streets are dirt and uneven. The residents I have met are cordial, perhaps appreciating the fact that anyone arriving there has gone through a certain amount of effort just to see the town. The overall effect: Silver City is one of my favorite ghost towns.

Located in the southwest corner of Idaho, Silver City sits in Owyhee (oh-WYE-hee) County, named, improbable as it may seem, for the Hawaiian fur trappers who

explored the area beginning in 1819. The mining history of Owyhee County, however, begins with the mad rush to War Eagle Mountain that created Silver City.

Prospectors had already found placer gold deposits along Idaho City's Grimes Creek in 1862. A party of twenty-nine miners from that area, led by Michael Jordan, decided to head out in May 1863 in search of the fabled (and perhaps mythical) "lost" Blue Bucket Diggings. What they found instead was placer gold along what came to be called Jordan Creek. Quartz ledges of primary gold deposits were discovered two months later. What the party had come upon was the second biggest mineral find in Idaho's history; the largest was found in the Coeur d'Alene area twenty years later (see the Wallace entry, pages 216–223). Soon the area was swarming with miners, and freight routes were extended from both year-old Boise

The Stoddard Mansion in Silver City may not compare in size with other mansions in the American West, but it holds its own when it comes to gingerbread trim.

Silver City's Idaho Hotel is a ghost town lover's dream: historic, authentic, and just rustic enough to make a night's stay unforgettable.

Present-day guests at Silver City's Idaho Hotel enter the past even as they check in. The Debold Safe behind the counter dates from about 1876. The guest ledger on the counter is an original to the hotel.

The Wells Fargo office inside the Idaho Hotel has, atop the agent's desk, a telegraph key, a jar battery to power the telegraph, a ledger, and a large scale.

City to the north and Oregon's Jordan Valley to the west. Silver City and several other towns were born, including Ruby City, a now-vanished community that was at one time larger than Silver City. Ruby City served as the first Owyhee County seat until that honor was moved to burgeoning Silver City in 1867.

Silver City eventually featured a population of around twenty-five hundred people and seventy-five businesses. The hills surrounding town had more than two hundred mines, but it soon became apparent that the real wealth of Silver City lay within the big hill to the east: War Eagle Mountain. The biggest strike there came in 1865 with the discovery of the Poorman Mine, so named because the discoverers knew they lacked the capital necessary to work it. The Poorman was unusual in that it yielded an amalgam of both gold and silver chloride, the latter appearing with a crimson tint. The color was dubbed Ruby Silver. Some of the Poorman Ruby Silver crystals were displayed at the 1866 Paris Exposition, winning a gold medal.

A telegraph line, Idaho Territory's first, was extended to Silver City from Winnemucca, Nevada, in 1874 and from Silver City to Boise a year later. Telephone service came in the 1880s, followed by electricity in 1903. At its mining peak, the Silver City Range contained more than sixty mills processing ore, with an estimated production of at least sixty million dollars, principally in silver, retrieved from area mines.

The peak years were over by the turn of the twentieth century, and the town's population took a dive after World War I, although some mining continued into the 1930s. Silver City declined sufficiently enough that the county seat was moved in 1934 to its present site at Murphy, which had something that eluded Silver City: a railroad connection to the world. Silver City's landmark Idaho Hotel shut its doors in about 1942, and the post office closed in 1943. In that same decade, the nearly empty community suffered a nearly fatal indignity: The electrical transmission lines were removed.

Ed Jagels purchased the Idaho Hotel in 1972 and reopened it for business, using a twelve-volt generator for power. He was a complete believer in the renaissance of Silver City and spent the rest of his life making it happen. I first met Jagels in 1998, three years before his death, and at that time his spirit and enthusiasm were infectious. Roger and Jerri Nelson bought the hotel from Jagels and have continued to make improvements to it (such as adding modern toilets with a septic system), without compromising the history or charm of the great building.

Today, Silver City is on the National Register of Historic Places, which means that property owners cannot build new buildings and can only make repairs on existing ones. About fifty families live there in the summer, and in the winter a watchman looks after the town. Silver City is alive and very much worth exploring.

WALKING AND DRIVING AROUND SILVER CITY

As you enter town, a sign cautions you to respect that this is an occupied town of private buildings. On the reverse side of that sign is a map that most visitors don't see until they're on the way out. It shows principal streets and the location of the cemetery.

You will enter town on Jordan Street after crossing Jordan Creek. On the southwest corner of Jordan and Avalanche streets is the former Owyhee County Office Building, now a gift shop. Directly across the street is the Idaho Hotel, a rambling structure that is, simply, one of the finest ghost town buildings in the American West. The Idaho Hotel is actually an amalgam of seven different buildings, the oldest of which is the 1866 three-story west wing, which was disassembled and loaded onto skids and sleds and dragged through snow to Silver City from short-lived Ruby City. That town stood where the road now turns toward Jordan Valley a half-mile west of Silver City. Inside the hotel, open for both meals and overnight accommodations, are a saloon-dining area, a Wells Fargo office, an elegant parlor, and eighteen rooms for guests, including the luxurious Empire Room, where I enjoyed a night surrounded by the nineteenth century.

Behind the hotel and straddling Jordan Creek is the 1869 Masonic Hall, a two-story structure that was originally built as a planing mill.

If you walk south from the hotel's porch, you'll be on Avalanche Street, which features the aforementioned former county office building, the Knapp Drug Store, and, on the corner of Avalanche and Washington streets, the Lippincott Building, which contained a doctor's office. More of the town's enchanting buildings extend down Washington, including the former Odd Fellows Hall; the Getchell Drug Store and Post Office, which has a fully-equipped dentist's office in the rear; and, across the street, the 1866 furniture store and vegetable market, which is a wooden building covered in pressed tin that has also served as a brewery and soda works (there's a natural spring in the basement); a bowling alley; and the Sommercamp Saloon.

One of the most graceful churches in the Mountain West, Silver City's Our Lady of Tears Catholic Church has undergone extensive restoration.

The Silver Slipper Saloon and the next-door Getchell Drug Store and Post Office in Silver City are privately owned and closed to the public. Be sure to peer through the drugstore windows to see the memorabilia within.

The rear section of the Getchell Drug Store features a fully equipped dentist's office.

Beyond the furniture store are the Hoffer and Miller Meat Market (now a private residence), the former Hawes Bazaar (a general store), and a one-time barbershop and bathhouse.

Across the street from these structures is a unique sight: a large beer vat turned into a tiny building with a miniature saloon scene inside it. Will Hawes, a lifelong Silver City resident who died in 1968 at ninety-one years of age, crafted the unusual piece.

On the north side of town off of Morning Star Street are three more of Silver City's best buildings: the 1892 Idaho Standard School, the 1898 Our Lady of Tears Catholic Church (which served as St. James Episcopal Church until it was sold to the Catholic Diocese of Boise in 1928), and the 1870 Stoddard Mansion, which features an almost stupefying amount of gingerbread trim.

The two Silver City cemeteries, one public and the other for Masons and Odd Fellows, stand west of town on a steep hill. The route is quite rough and definitely requires a high-clearance vehicle, but the distance is only .2 of a mile, so you can easily walk there from town, starting three buildings west from the former county building. A sign points the way.

An elaborate cut stone wall in the Masonic and Odd Fellows cemetery surrounds two graves for the children of W. F. and Mary Sommercamp (the one-time owners of the Sommercamp Saloon on Washington Street). Son Frederick died in 1870 at five months; daughter Annie lived only fourteen months and died in 1874.

WHEN YOU GO

Silver City is 67 miles southwest of Boise. From Idaho City, proceed 36 miles south-west to Boise via Idaho Highway 21. From Boise, take Interstate 84 west 16 miles to Nampa. Follow Idaho Highway 45, which joins Idaho Highway 78, south from Nampa for 27 miles to Murphy. Southeast of Murphy 4.5 miles is Silver City Road, which in 18.8 miles takes you to a junction only .5 of a mile from Silver City. Turn left (a right takes you to Jordan Valley, Oregon) and proceed into town, passing two stone powderhouses on your left.

Note: The last 12 miles are on a twisting, mountainous road. In dry weather, the road is quite good, but I would nevertheless recommend a high-clearance vehicle.

6

MONTANA

G H O S T S   O F

BIG SKY COUNTRY

MONTANA IS THE NATION'S FOURTH-LARGEST STATE. Fortunately, the best ghost towns are all situated in its southwestern quarter. That's also the location of some of the state's most scenic areas. *Montana* comes from a Latin word meaning "mountainous," which aptly describes the section you'll be exploring.

Montana was admitted to the Union in 1889, eight months prior to Idaho and Wyoming. Its state motto is *Oro y Plata*, Spanish for "Gold and Silver," although much of the state's wealth came not from those minerals but from copper. When inventions like the telephone created numerous uses for copper, Montanans found their real bonanza.

Montana's ghost towns range from the protected (Bannack and Garnet) to the commercial (Virginia City and Nevada City) to the almost deserted (Comet and Elkhorn). Each is a delight to visit and photograph.

Note: At the end of the chapter, you'll be only a couple of hours' drive on Interstate 90 from Wallace and Burke, Idaho, which are included in this chapter on Montana as a ghost town bonus.

The Bannack Masonic Lodge and schoolhouse, one of the first Masonic temples erected in Montana, was built in the Greek Revival style. The Masons offered the lower floor to the people of Bannack as a schoolhouse, and the citizens gratefully accepted.

A dressmaker's form is the only inhabitant on the second story of Garnet's J. K. Wells Hotel.

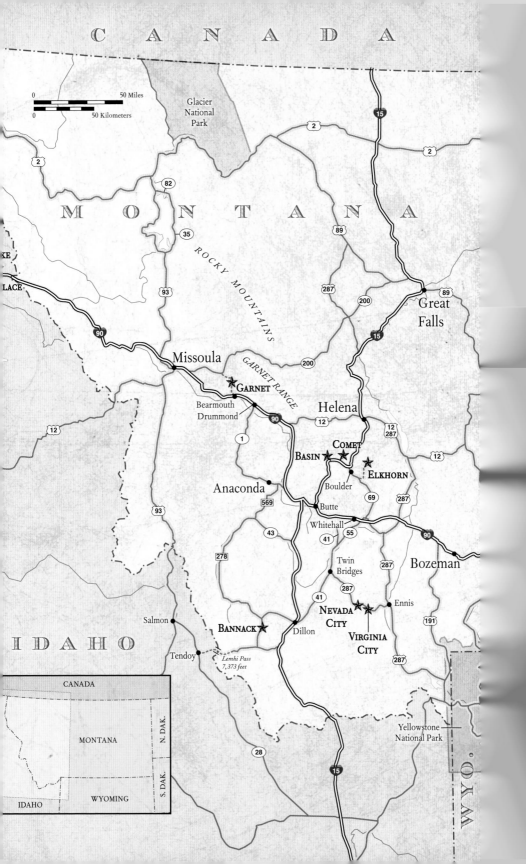

BANNACK

Bannack is one of the Mountain West's great ghost towns, featuring more than four dozen well-preserved buildings, some of which contain artifacts of antiquity.

The town of Bannock was born not long after a group of Colorado-based prospectors (called Pikes Peakers), led by John White and William Eades, found gold along Grasshopper Creek in July 1862. It was named for the nearby Bannock Indians, but the U.S. Postal Service, when granting a post office the following year, mistook the "o" for an "a," and "Bannack" it became. The community, which reached a population of four hundred in a matter of weeks, was the first major gold camp in Montana, with an estimated half million dollars of ore shipped by the end of 1862.

Bannack's prominence was challenged in 1864, when promising gold strikes were found along Last Chance Gulch (later Helena) and Alder Gulch (later Virginia City—see following entry, pages 194–197). Bannack and Virginia City, a mere fifty miles apart as the crow flies, became inextricably linked early in their history by the Vigilance Committee and the Innocents.

When twenty-first-century people think of "vigilante justice," it usually carries a negative connotation. And "innocents"? Certainly they must be law-abiding people. In Bannack and Virginia City, those notions were reversed completely.

Henry Plummer came to Bannack in its earliest days. Appearing to be a trustworthy and earnest fellow, Plummer was selected by townspeople as sheriff. What they did not know was that Plummer was only three years out California's San Quentin prison. He organized a group of similar chaps into a clandestine gang of road agents, or highwaymen, named the Innocents, so called because they swore to their guiltlessness of any wrongdoing. This gang of blackguards began a reign of terror in both Bannack and Virginia City, particularly on helpless travelers en route between the two towns. They are believed to have robbed and/or murdered more than a hundred people in eight short months.

In response to this mayhem, a secret band of stalwart citizens, calling themselves the Vigilance Committee, or the Vigilantes, vowed to restore order and

MONTANA

The Hotel Meade was erected in Bannack in 1875 as the Beaverhead County Courthouse. It became a hotel in 1890, nine years after the county seat was moved to Dillon, twenty-five miles east of Bannack.

justice. They pursued the road agents and, within a little more than a month, caught, "tried," and hanged twenty-four of them, including, as the result of a condemned man's testimony, Sheriff Henry Plummer himself. When Sidney Edgerton, appointed by President Abraham Lincoln to be Chief Justice of the Idaho Territory (which then included Idaho and Montana), arrived in Bannack two months after the hanging spree, he concluded that the Vigilantes had done exactly what was necessary at the time. A year later, Bannack citizens, now four thousand strong, chose Edgerton to journey to Washington, D.C., to petition for a division of the Idaho Territory. Not only was he successful, but he became the first governor of the Territory of Montana. Legal authority was firmly in place in Bannack, the territory's first capital.

Bannack, however, held that distinction for only seven months, when the first territorial legislature voted in December 1864 to move the capital to Virginia City. Bannack was on a slow path of decline, as other gold strikes eclipsed Montana's first rush.

Mining at Bannack was primarily of secondary deposits—the retrieval of gold from streams and riverbanks. This was done first by panning, then by hydraulic mining, and finally by dredging. Each technique is, in a way, a bit more desperate than the method before, since gold seekers are essentially going over the same area, with newer technology, trying to find the precious metal that the previous attempts missed. The easy placering was over in a couple of years. Hydraulicking continued into the turn of the twentieth century, and dredging operations, the first in the United States, lasted from 1895 until about 1905. Smalltime hard-rock operations kept Bannack alive into the 1940s, after which the town was essentially abandoned.

Although some subsequent vandalizing took place in Bannack, concerned Montanans began to work to save the townsite not long after it became a ghost. When the town was finally turned over to the State of Montana in 1954, a principal stipulation was that it was to be preserved as a relic, not turned into a tourist mecca. You will be pleased at what remains.

WALKING AROUND BANNACK

Bannack today has a true feel of entering the past. You will pay a park fee and be given a walking tour brochure, which is free unless you decide to keep it.

When the Nez Perce attack did not materialize (see photo caption, page 192), Preacher William "Brother Van" Van Orsdel used the occasion to encourage the people of Bannack to show gratitude by erecting a church: The result was this Methodist church, built in 1877.

I was talking to a group of tourists in Virginia City who had just been to Bannack and were very disappointed because the buildings were closed up. They preferred Virginia City and its tourist shops and felt Bannack would have been more worthwhile if you could go inside the buildings. Here's what I didn't have the heart to tell them: Folks, you can go inside most of the structures; you just have to turn the doorknobs. Park rangers merely ask you to close the doors behind you.

Since you'll have a walking tour brochure, I'll mention only a few highlights. One is the unusual 1874 Masonic Lodge. The masons helped the community by donating the ground floor of their lodge to serve as a public school. The Masons had their meetings on the second floor in a lodge that still features Masonic paraphernalia, which you can view through glass partitions.

The winding staircase of Bannack's county courthouse (later the Hotel Meade) was used in August 1877, when women and children were sent inside "the fortress" because of a feared Nez Perce Indian attack. Children were rumored to have been ready to hide in the courthouse's large safes. The attack never occurred.

Across the street from the schoolhouse/lodge is the most impressive structure in town, the two-story, brick, 1875 Beaverhead County Courthouse, which served until 1881, when the county seat was moved, after a contentious election, to Dillon, where it still resides.

After almost a decade of standing empty, the courthouse was remodeled into the Hotel Meade by Dr. John Singleton Meade. This upscale hostelry operated off and on during every period of Bannack's prosperity until the 1940s.

Next door to the courthouse/hotel is Cyrus Skinner's Saloon, a favorite hangout of Henry Plummer's road agents. After the highwaymen were dispatched by the Vigilantes, Skinner, too, was hanged for his association with Plummer and his gang. Later, the building became a general mercantile.

Across the street and down a bit from Skinner's Saloon is Chrisman's Store, and, behind it, Bannack's two jails, the first ever constructed in Montana. From the smaller of the jails, one can look through the bars to see, up Hangman's Gulch north of town, a reconstruction of the gallows that Sheriff Henry Plummer ordered built—the same gallows from which he eventually swayed when discovered to be a leader of the Innocents.

If you walk up to those gallows, you can take a path over to the Pioneer Cemetery, used from 1860 until about 1880. A later cemetery, containing more than sixty graves and many wooden fences, is .4 of a mile beyond the turnoff to Bannack on the east side of the road to Dillon.

On the east side of Bannack are two more buildings of note. The first is the 1877 Methodist church, Bannack's first house of worship. It was constructed as a result of the determination of William Van Orsdel, known affectionately as Brother Van, who charmed and cajoled Bannack's citizens into contributing funds to erect his church.

Immediately west of the church stands the 1866 or 1867 Roe/Graves House, the first frame house built in Bannack. It is also the town's largest house, with a dozen rooms.

WHEN YOU GO

Bannack is 25 miles west of Dillon. Take Interstate 15's Exit 59, which is 4 miles southwest of Dillon's Exit 63, and follow Montana Highway 278 west for 17 miles to a junction with Bannack Bench Road, where a sign directs you to Bannack, 3.7 miles south.

Bannack can also be reached from Idaho, by taking Idaho Highway 28 about 20 miles southeast of Salmon at Tendoy. From Tendoy, Agency Creek Road (also known by the cumbersome title of Lewis and Clark National Back Country Byway and Adventure Road) goes into Montana via Lemhi Pass. Bannack is 46 miles northeast of Tendoy.

VIRGINIA CITY

Lovers of Western history in general and ghost towns in particular owe a tremendous debt of gratitude to Charles and Sue Bovey. In 1944, they bought more than one hundred Virginia City buildings in an effort to save the historic frontier town. As a result of their efforts, the town was designated a National Historic Monument in 1961. As great as their contributions to Virginia City were, however, the Boveys would do even more ambitious things in Nevada City (see following entry, pages 198–201).

In May 1863, a group of prospectors from Bannack (see previous entry, page 188) intended to see what the Yellowstone River might offer, but the Crow Indians "encouraged" them to go back the way they came. In Alder Gulch, only about fifty miles from Bannack, the prospectors found potentially promising placer deposits. Sworn to secrecy, they returned to Bannack for supplies. Secrecy is relative: When they returned to their claims, nearly two hundred men accompanied them, and the rush at Alder Gulch was on.

By the next year, a string of camps along Alder Gulch, proclaimed a "fourteen-mile city," had a total population of ten thousand people. Virginia City was the largest, followed by neighboring Nevada City.

Virginia City's name came as a result of a kind of compromise. The Civil War was in full force in 1863, and the miners were fairly evenly split between Union and Confederate sympathizers. The Rebels wanted to name the town Varina City after Jefferson Davis' wife, but a judge with Union leanings, and with considerable wisdom, decided upon Virginia City, named for a state that had divided Civil War sympathies as well.

The early history of Virginia City was marked by the same lawlessness that plagued Bannack. Bannack's rogue sheriff, Henry Plummer, was the de facto power in Virginia City as well, until the Vigilance Committee put an end to the chaos. For more on those events, read the Bannack entry (pages 188–193).

The gold rush at Alder Gulch was still booming as Bannack's placers were playing out. Although Bannack was chosen as the first territorial capital, seven months later Virginia City took the honor. The town proudly held that banner until 1875, when the capital was moved to its present site, Helena. By that time, Virginia City seemed to be in serious decline, but in 1899 dredging of Alder Gulch began.

Virginia City's Masonic Temple (second building from right) was erected for the then-huge sum of thirty thousand dollars, making it the most expensive edifice in Montana in 1867. To the left of the temple is the Pfouts and Russell Building, built in 1865.

Six huge dredges pulled out nine million dollars in gold before being retired in the mid-1920s. Dredging evidence is obvious today along the highway from Nevada City west to the town of Alder.

With the end of large-scale mining along Alder Gulch, much of Virginia City dried up, even though it remained, and still is, the seat of Madison County. The business district was heading toward terminal decay—only to be saved by the efforts of Charles and Sue Bovey.

WALKING AND DRIVING AROUND VIRGINIA CITY

Wallace Street, the highway that runs through town, features most of Virginia City's historic buildings. On the west end of town is the visitors' center, housed in a railroad depot that was moved from Harrison, Montana, in 1964. An excellent walking tour map available there will give you plenty of historical details. The map is set up to begin at the depot.

Of the sixty-six sites highlighted by the tour map, by my count thirty-eight are Virginia City originals. The others were either moved to the community, like the depot, or are reconstructions. Unlike Bannack, where nothing is for sale except for a few items in the visitors' center, Virginia City has restaurants, saloons, an old-time photo shop, an active theater, lodgings, and a train that offers rides to

Charles and Sue Bovey, who purchased and saved Virginia City, turned the 1899 building on the left into the Wells Fargo Coffee House in 1947. The adjacent building is a 1950 reconstruction. The other structures down the street date from 1863.

Nevada City. But the town also has several museumlike attractions, such as the Sauerbier Blacksmith Shop, the barbershop, and the E. L. Smith Store.

East of the main business district is the 1918 Thompson-Hickman Museum (and public library), which offers an eclectic selection of artifacts from the town's history, including one truly grisly item: the club foot of George Lane, one of five road agents hanged in 1864 by the Vigilance Committee (his foot, exhumed, later proved which grave in Boot Hill was his).

Speaking of Boot Hill, Virginia City's two cemeteries stand on a hill above town. From the museum, head north from Wallace on Spencer Street and follow the signs; the tiny Boot Hill Cemetery, which was abandoned not long after the road agents' burials (respectable people didn't want their loved ones near such nefarious characters), is up to the left, while the New Cemetery, which replaced Boot Hill, is to the right. A road across the saddle of the hill connects the two, so it doesn't matter which you visit first.

Idaho Street, one block south of Wallace, features a variety of houses from the crudest hand-hewn log cabin to modest wood-frame residences and elegant Victorians.

Also on Idaho Street are two very different churches, the handsome 1902 to 1904 St. Paul's Episcopal and the incredibly austere 1875 Methodist church, which has no front-facing windows, no steeple, and a stucco exterior scored to look like stone.

E. L. Smith opened a dry goods store in 1880 in what had been a billiard hall built in Virginia City in 1863. Much of the original merchandise is still on display. The store is reputed to have had the first "show windows" in Montana.

Left: Ribbons and spools of thread stand in their original case in the E. L. Smith Store.

WHEN YOU GO

Virginia City is 13.6 miles west of Ennis on Montana Highway 287. Or from Bannack, drive 25 miles east to Dillon. From Dillon, head 29 miles northeast to Twin Bridges on Montana Highway 41. From there, take Highway 287 for 30 miles to Virginia City. You will pass through Nevada City 1.5 miles before reaching Virginia City.

NEVADA CITY

Nevada City shows even more evidence of the efforts of Charles and Sue Bovey than Virginia City (see preceding entry, pages 194–197). While the Boveys were purchasing portions of that town in the 1940s to preserve it, they were also buying a series of buildings in various old towns and ranches and having them placed on the fairgrounds of their hometown of Great Falls, Montana. When that community needed more fairground space, the Boveys had their entire "Old Town" exhibit moved, in 1959, to their latest acquisition, Nevada City.

In the 1860s, Nevada City was essentially a suburb, at about one-fifth the size, of Virginia City. They were linked by the same source of income, Alder Gulch. People moved freely from one town to the other for commerce, entertainment, and services; they also suffered the same violence brought on by Bannack's Henry Plummer and had the eventual retribution by the Vigilance Committee.

When Alder Gulch mining faded by 1868, Nevada City virtually disappeared, while Virginia City merely declined to a shell of its former self. The second life that Virginia City received in 1899 when dredging operations began had no effect upon Nevada City: By that time, the latter town was mostly a memory.

Enter Charles and Sue Bovey and the renaissance of Nevada City.

WALKING AROUND NEVADA CITY

Several "pioneer towns"—places where historic buildings have been brought together to be preserved and enjoyed—exist in the West. South Park City, Colorado, mentioned earlier in this book (page 44–47), is one of the best, and Nevada City is in the same class. Of the sixty-nine buildings I counted on the site, only nine are original to Nevada City. But virtually all others are documented, historic structures that were carefully disassembled, transported, and reassembled with expert care from sites all over Montana. Virtually all of them would no longer exist if it were not for the Boveys. The overall effect is a charming, interesting town worthy of being in the movies—and it has been, including *Little Big Man* and *Missouri Breaks*, along with several television programs.

You will be given a walking guide and map upon paying an appropriate admission fee (which covers two days, if you wish to return). The guide begins,

On the north end of Nevada City's California Street stand, from left to right, the Parmeter House, once the home of Sheridan's mayor, O. F. Parmeter; a residence from the vanished town of Iron Rod; and the former Twin Bridges Schoolhouse.

From 1867 until 1873, this tiny schoolhouse served Twin Bridges, northwest of Nevada City. Note that one of the vocabulary words on the blackboard is, appropriately, "Vigilante."

Nevada City's Sedman House, which stands dramatically at the end of Brewery Street, was built in 1873 in nearby Junction City.

as did the one at Virginia City, with the town's depot, one of Nevada City's few unauthentic structures. It is a replica of a depot in Minnesota.

Many of Nevada City's buildings contain portions of the huge collections of memorabilia that the Boveys accumulated, so visitors really can have a nineteenth-century experience. Some of the better examples are found in the Dry Goods Store, the Cheap Cash Store, the Applebound and Crabb Store (used in *Little Big Man*—Dustin Hoffman's character was Jack Crabb), Sullivan's Saddlery, the Sedman House, the schoolhouse, and, especially, the Music Hall, where you will find an astonishing assortment of mechanical musical devices.

To visit the Nevada City Cemetery, drive .2 of a mile west of town, turn north, and proceed another .2 of a mile to the cemetery entrance, where you will see wrought-iron and wooden fences and several headstones. On your way to the cemetery, you'll pass the elaborate 1895 Guinan House, which was moved from nearby Laurin and which is not, at this writing, open to visitors.

WHEN YOU GO

Nevada City is 1.5 miles west of Virginia City on Montana Highway 287.

The Elkhorn Barber Shop (left), now located in Nevada City, once stood across the street from the two halls still standing in Elkhorn (see photo, page 209). Next door is Sullivan's Saddlery, where renowned Western artist Charles Russell once hung out as a youth in its original location, Fort Benton. The small log building beyond is an original to Nevada City: its jail.

Nevada City's Applebound and Crabb Store, which was featured in the film *Little Big Man* (Dustin Hoffman played Jack Crabb), was originally an outbuilding on a ranch near Ennis, east of Virginia City. Beyond the store is a building now used to display assay equipment.

BASIN

Basin is a minor site that wouldn't be in this book except that it is so close to Comet, the following entry (pages 204–207). As long as you're going to Comet, take a look at Basin.

A sign placed before you enter Basin states that you are in approximately the center of a mining district that extended from Butte to Helena. It also says that the area's ore was initially sent to smelters as far away as Wales and Germany. It fails to mention, however, that the journey became unnecessary when towns such as Basin, right down the road, and Wickes, about ten miles away, came into being. Basin and Wickes had smelters.

Basin, originally called Basin City, was the site of modest placer gold deposits found in 1880. It was gold hard-rock mines, along with silver and lead deposits, however, that held the real promise for Basin, which had a peak population of about fifteen hundred. Gold mining and smelting operations kept the town alive through the Silver Crash of 1893, with production lasting into the 1920s before shutting down, partially as the result of a stock fraud.

WALKING AND DRIVING AROUND BASIN

One thing to notice as you enter town on Basin Street is the variety of materials used in the town's structures. In fact, they chronicle the major steps in the gentrification of a community: You'll see buildings of hand-hewn timber, cut stone, milled lumber, and brick. On your left is an attractive, wood-frame Catholic church with an unusual diagonal entrance and bell tower. On Quartz Avenue, which heads north from Basin Street, is the two-story, clapboard Basin Grade School, featuring a bell tower complete with bell.

West of town are the remains of the 1903 Glass Brothers Smelter: a large stack, a long flue, and stone foundations. Across the interstate from the smelter ruins are mill foundations.

The Rainville Memorial Cemetery is east of town. Return toward the interstate .4 of a mile from the middle of town. Turn left on Cataract Creek Road, and angle left almost immediately onto a road that goes north .2 of a mile to the graveyard.

The large stack and its flue are the principal remains of the Glass Brothers Smelter in Basin.

WHEN YOU GO

From Nevada City, head west on Montana Highway 287 for 28 miles to Twin Bridges. Take Montana Highway 41 and then Montana Highway 55 for 28 miles north to Whitehall, where you join Interstate 90. From there, it's 22 miles west to Butte, which features a remarkable, decaying, historic downtown.

From Butte, take Interstate 15 northeast for 27 miles to Exit 156, Basin.

COMET

Comet is a wonderful, genuine ghost town, the third best in Montana, after Bannack and Garnet. It features more than three dozen wooden buildings, including a huge mill, a two-story mill-workers' and miners' dormitory, and numerous wood or log cabins.

Comet came to life in 1883, nine years after silver ore was located in the area but not substantially developed. The town of Wickes, four miles north, smelted the Comet Mine's ore by way of a tramway. Its most prosperous days were during the 1880s, when the town could boast of a population of three hundred, but the Silver Crash hit hard in 1893 and it was deserted by the end of World War I.

It was not deserted for long. A second mining operation began in the 1920s; a new mill, the one still standing at Comet, was built in 1926, and the population returned to its pre-1893 level. That prosperity ended with the beginning of World War II. Many mines in the American West, such as Comet, never reopened after World War II because an industrial surge for consumer goods offered jobs in manufacturing that paid better wages and were far less dangerous than mining. Eventually, more restrictive mine safety standards made reopening old mines prohibitively expensive.

Here is an excellent example of ghost town safety: Do not attempt to climb the stairs of the Comet boardinghouse or you might be the last person who does.

Opposite: Comet's boardinghouse is one of the few two-story structures in residential Comet. As you can see, it badly needs restoration or at least propping up.

A nearby forest fire gave Comet's mill, dormitory, and stack an eerie glow in this early morning photograph.

WALKING AND DRIVING AROUND COMET

Your first glimpse of Comet will be of two ore chutes on your left as you approach the site. You then round a corner, and Comet stands in a panorama before you. Across the draw to the east is the Comet Mine's last mill and its two-story dormitory, both clad in tin sheets. The mill's tailings were removed in 2000 as an environmental hazard, so the mill stands there in an eerie parklike setting.

To your immediate left are the general store, several residences, a two-story boardinghouse, and many mine-related structures. Up on the hill behind these buildings are at least a dozen miners' shacks, standing in various states of decay. Amid them is an occupied residence, and I, for one, am very glad they are there. I was watched each time I have been to Comet; with that vigilance, Comet should last much longer than if it were abandoned. But what Comet really needs is to be purchased and protected by the State of Montana.

Left: Unlike the pickup in Belmont, Nevada (see photo, page 8), this Chevrolet in Comet is well past restoration. Behind stand miners' cabins in various states of decay.

WHEN YOU GO

From Basin, take Interstate 15 east 3.2 miles to Exit 160, High Ore Road. Follow High Ore Road over the Boulder River, cross a cattle guard, and head north for 4.5 miles to Comet.

ELKHORN

Photographs of Elkhorn taken in the 1970s show an extensive townsite with dozens of deserted wooden buildings. Unfortunately, time, weather, fire, and capitalism have reduced it to what it is today: an amalgam of ruins, modern occupied structures, a certain amount of junk—and two of the best buildings in the ghost town West.

Gravity and Montana's harsh winters helped some deserted structures collapse. Fire destroyed one of the town's premier residences. But several of the better buildings, including the two-story Grand Hotel, were dismantled and sold for the valuable siding or for reassembly elsewhere. If it weren't for Gillian Hall and Fraternity Hall, which constitute the smallest state park in Montana, Elkhorn wouldn't be included in this book. But every ghost town enthusiast simply must see these two buildings.

The rush to Elkhorn began when Swiss prospector Peter Wys found rich silver ore in 1870. He died only two years later, however, and it was Anton M. Holter, a miner from another of Montana's booming camps, Virginia City, who made the fortune from Wys' claim beginning in 1875. His Elkhorn Mine became a solid silver producer, which, when sold in 1888 to a British corporation for one-half million dollars, was bringing in thirty thousand dollars monthly. That corporation improved the mining and milling processes and recouped their investment within two years.

But they only had three more years of prosperity because the Silver Crash of 1893 was the beginning of the end for Elkhorn. The once-vibrant town of twenty-five hundred people lost more than 75 percent of its population in two months.

Limited mining, along with a reworking of old tailings, occurred sporadically until 1951, but the post office only held on until 1924.

WALKING AND DRIVING AROUND ELKHORN

Except for the two halls, Elkhorn is all on private property, but you can see almost everything from the road. I'd recommend leaving your car in the parking area just south of town, where there is also a public toilet and an interpretive sign. Walk into town and notice the posted signs that either tell what purpose a structure served in the community or what used to occupy a now-vacant site.

Two of the most photogenic and famous ghost town buildings of the Mountain West are Elkhorn's Gillian Hall (left) and Fraternity Hall.

The buildings that brought you to Elkhorn are hard to miss: The 1880s Gillian Hall and the 1893 Fraternity Hall dominate the town. At this writing, you can walk into each building (but be sure to secure the doors when you leave). The older Gillian Hall featured one commercial enterprise after another on the main floor, while the upstairs had a saloon and dance hall. Its neighbor, Fraternity Hall, was built through donations to be a community center, complete with a first-story auditorium, featuring a proscenium arch stage for theatrical productions and dance bands. On the second floor was a meeting place for various lodge groups. The building was officially opened, with the Cornish Glee Club and the Elkhorn

Brass Band leading the celebration, on July 4, 1893. The euphoria was short-lived: In November of that year came the calamitous drop in silver prices and the emptying of Elkhorn.

Directly across the street from the halls stands a white clapboard structure that served as the town's general store well after the peak years of Elkhorn's prosperity.

Beyond the halls are several vacant lots and small cabins. At the north end of town, closed to the public, are the considerable remains of the Elkhorn Mine's milling remnants.

Elkhorn's cemetery is .9 of a mile away from town, so you might want to return to your car. Follow the main road north from town as it winds around to the east and then to the south (a sign points the way). For part of your journey, you'll be on an old railroad bed.

One of the first headstones at the cemetery is for Peter Wys, the original discoverer of Elkhorn's riches. His monument was placed in 1912 as a commemoration, forty years after his death, of his importance to the community. The graveyard, which is still in use, features several dozen markers of various materials: wood, marble, and at least one of pot metal. (These metal markers, which were usually purchased from mail-order catalogues, look like dark marble, but if you tap them with a coin, you will hear that they are metal.) You will also find several markers of young children who died in 1889 during a diphtheria outbreak.

On your way back to the townsite, stop for a moment to survey the town and, especially, the huge workings of the Elkhorn Mine's mill. What you could not see from street level spreads out before you.

WHEN YOU GO

From Comet, return to Interstate 15 and drive 4.3 miles northeast to Exit 164. Follow Montana Highway 69 through Boulder (make a one-block detour west on Third Avenue to see the handsome 1888 Jefferson County Courthouse) for 7.2 miles to Forest Service Road 517, which is marked for Elkhorn. In 3.1 miles, turn left onto Forest Service Road 258, which in 8.2 miles will take you to Elkhorn. As you near the townsite, you'll see a stone powderhouse on your right, followed immediately on your left by a huge tailings pile with a rusting boiler at its base.

GARNET

Garnet's prosperity came late in the Montana mining game. Although placer gold deposits were discovered in the 1870s in the Garnet Range, the country was so remote that prospectors looked elsewhere for easier strikes. The discovery of plentiful silver in western Montana and northern Idaho caused miners to abandon questionable gold claims and rush to get in on those bonanzas. But with the Silver Crash of 1893, miners looked again at older gold claims that had been staked but abandoned.

Many of those miners returned to the Garnet Range, where a small settlement was built around a stamp mill erected in 1895 by Armistead L. Mitchell. The community was originally called Mitchell in his honor, but by 1897, the year the town received its post office, it was known as Garnet, named for the semiprecious, rubylike mineral. The town's population swelled to about a thousand by the end of the nineteenth century.

Garnet was unusual in that it was a peaceful community, more of a family place rather than a rowdy town of ne'er-do-wells. Although it had the usual

saloons and brothels, it also featured refinements such as a doctor's office, a candy store, family residences instead of miners' shacks, and a miners' union hall. That union hall was pivotal to the orderly atmosphere in Garnet: Every miner in Garnet was a member of the union, and disputes were resolved by the union. Miscreants either changed their ways or left town. There was a jail, but it served principally as a drunk tank.

The dusty dining room of the J. K. Wells Hotel in Garnet is exactly what ghost town seekers hope to find instead of empty, vandalized buildings. In its heyday around the turn of the twentieth century, the Wells was considered quite luxurious.

This is your first view as you walk from the parking lot to Garnet. Prominent in the lower center is Kelly's Saloon. Next door stands Frank Davey's store. The large, three-story building in the right background is the J. K. Wells Hotel.

The last resident of Garnet, Frank Davey, lived in the kitchen of the Wells Hotel. When he died in 1947, everything in the hotel was sold. Items on display are representative of what was once in a typical hotel kitchen.

Garnet's boom was short. By 1905, the population had shrunk to less than two hundred, and a fire in 1912 caused many holdouts to leave. Only a few people remained after the United States entered World War I because war-related jobs were steadier and paid better than haphazard gold mining work.

During the Great Depression, Garnet saw a modest rebirth. Because employment opportunities were scarce, and because the price of gold had more than doubled to thirty-five dollars per ounce, about 250 people returned to rework old mines and waste dumps with improved technology that retrieved gold that earlier, cruder processing had missed. Then came World War II and the enactment of Law 208, closing mines that were not directly assisting the war effort. In 1942, the year the post office closed, the sole resident was Frank Davey, owner of the town's last store. Sent a document by the Internal Revenue Service requiring him to sign in front of a witness, he gazed into his mirror, signed in both places, and noted to the IRS that he was the only resident of Garnet, Montana.

Davey died in 1947, and the auction of his effects served as the beginning of Garnet as a true ghost town.

WALKING AROUND GARNET

You will park your car in a lot that is about a six-minute walk from Garnet (a separate handicapped lot is closer to the townsite). You will be stepping back in time, and when you come to an overlook of Garnet, you might even gasp: You'll be looking at more than a dozen log and wood-frame buildings under roof—and you won't be seeing them all.

Immediately prior to entering the townsite are toilets, drinking water, and a stand with an excellent tour brochure. A few buildings in town are private, but most others are open for your inspection. Be sure to walk into Kelly's Saloon, the first building on your left; Frank Davey's Store and annex, next door to the saloon; and, across the street, Ole Dahl's Saloon, a 1938 building from Garnet's last hurrah, which now serves as a visitors' center. The biggest treat comes from exploring the 1897 J. K. Wells Hotel. You can enter almost every room, all the way to the third floor.

Residences, the original post office, a blacksmith's shop, and the town jail fan out across the meadow behind the center of town. The privately owned schoolhouse stands west of the jail.

A separate walking tour goes north from the parking lot to the Sierra Mine workings. A brochure for that interpretive trail is available at the trailhead.

WHEN YOU GO

Garnet can be reached from two directions. Tour buses and vehicles pulling trailers arrive from the north, turning south off Montana Highway 200 at a sign between mile markers 22 and 23. Garnet is 11 miles down that road.

The second route is for backroads-loving ghost town enthusiasts. Get off Interstate 90 at either the Drummond Exit, Exit 153 (from the east) or the Bearmouth Exit, Exit 138 (from the west), and follow the frontage road to Bear Gulch Road (10 miles from Drummond or 5.5 miles from Bearmouth).

This road, better with a high-clearance vehicle, proceeds through placer detritus on a road that, despite the narrow canyons and steep grades, is excellent in good weather. You'll pass historic mine workings and old cabins, because this is the route the Garnet pioneers took.

At 6.6 miles, the route splits. A longer, easier one goes right, while the original goes up First Chance Gulch, the more narrow, steep, and historic choice—and the only way I've gone in. You'll be at the Garnet parking area in 3.1 miles from the beginning of First Chance Gulch.

WALLACE, IDAHO

Wallace is not a ghost town. After all, the traffic of an elevated Interstate 90 runs above it. But Wallace, a remarkable remnant of an enormous mining boom, features an outstanding 1890s historic downtown district and belongs in this book the way Colorado's Central City does.

Mineral riches were discovered in the Coeur d'Alene Mining District in 1883, when prospector Andrew Pritchard found gold near what is now Murray, north of Wallace. A year later, gold was found much closer to Wallace at the Tiger and Poorman claims near Burke (see following entry, pages 224-225). But silver, not gold, was to provide the great riches of the Coeur d'Alene District, aptly known as the Silver Capital of the World. Between 1884 and 1968, the district produced 47 percent of the United States' silver, 30 percent of its lead, and 12 percent of its zinc. Mining continues to this day, with a yield of about forty million dollars annually.

The Northern Pacific Railroad Depot, built in 1902, is the logical place to begin your tour of downtown Wallace, Idaho.

In 1883, a self-titled Colonel Wallace staked a claim he called the Oreornogo, as in, one assumes, "ore or no go." It was a go: That claim became known as the Hecla, a huge producer. A year later, he purchased eighty acres of cedar trees and swamp, built a cabin on it, and called the modest spot Placer Center. His wife, Lucy, arrived the following year, and when the town of fourteen people applied for a post office, it was in the name of Wallace, with Lucy Wallace the first postmistress.

By 1886, Wallace had become a prosperous town of five hundred people surrounded by mining claims. A school for fifteen students opened that year, and a narrow gauge railroad arrived a year later. The silver rush attracted miners from Canada, Ireland, Germany, Italy, Finland, and Norway.

In 1890, a fire decimated Wallace's wooden downtown, but residents rebuilt immediately, this time—with one exception—using brick. It is those buildings that draw tourists to Wallace today.

Three years later, Wallace had to fight a different kind of disaster. The Silver Crash of 1893 crippled its economy, but, unlike many Western silver towns, Wallace survived, in part because of the enormous quantity of silver that was being produced.

The wisdom of the townspeople to rebuild with brick became evident in 1910, when a huge forest fire burned more than three million acres of northern Idaho and western Montana. Only the east end of Wallace was damaged. The fire, known as the Big Blowup, so threatened Wallace that women and children were evacuated by train to Missoula.

The most recent threat to Wallace's marvelous downtown came in the name of "progress." Wallace stands in a narrow canyon, and when the federal government routed Interstate 90 from Boston to Seattle, Wallace was directly in its path.

I remember driving from Seattle to Denver in 1991. My daughter and I were speeding along the interstate when something surreal happened. Signs slowed us down, routed us into a delightful downtown, and we came to a stop at a traffic light. After the light, we rejoined the highway and went on our way. Wallace was the last piece of the interstate puzzle, and the light at Bank and Seventh streets was the final stoplight on the entire interstate system. At that time, Wallace wags gave

The blinking yellow traffic light on historic Bank Street in Wallace replaced the last true stoplight in the entire United States interstate highway system.

The stationmaster's office inside the depot in Wallace features, from left, the stationmaster's hat, a dark red check writer, and a Western Electric Company candlestick phone, with a patent date of 1904.

these directions: "If you want to come here, drive all the interstates until you come to a traffic light. When you do, you're in Wallace."

The town was saved because forward-thinking citizens managed to have the downtown district placed on the National Register of Historic Places before Interstate 90 neared Wallace. As a result, one part of the federal government was protecting a community that another part wanted to destroy. Interstate 90 would have to avoid Wallace by going above it, not through it.

WALKING AND DRIVING AROUND WALLACE, IDAHO

The place to begin your tour of Wallace is the handsome 1902 Northern Pacific Railway Depot, located where Pine Street ends at Sixth Street. When the interstate came to Wallace, the depot was moved two hundred feet south for giant highway support columns. Inside the depot, now a museum, you can obtain a visitors' guide that will greatly increase your enjoyment of the town.

With your tour guide in hand, walk, rather than drive, around town. Many of the best buildings are on Bank Street, including the 1890 Rossi Insurance Building on the southeast corner of Bank and Sixth streets, which features a pressed metal turret that rises above the diagonal front entrance. That last traffic signal

on the interstate system, now merely blinking yellow, is a block east of the Rossi building at Seventh Street.

In the northwest corner of downtown, at Fifth and River streets, stands an American classic, the Wallace Carnegie Library, built in 1910 and 1911, one of only four operational Carnegie libraries remaining in Idaho.

West of the business district is a residential area that features numerous Victorian homes. Cedar Street, one block north of Bank, has a dozen houses well worth viewing.

One of Wallace's most outstanding attractions is not mentioned at all in the visitors' guide: the 1885 Nine Mile Cemetery. From the former railroad depot, take Sixth Street north under the interstate and follow Sixth out of town, where

The Sierra Silver Mine

The Sierra Silver Mine should more accurately be named the Sierra Would-Be Silver Mine, since, as our guide ruefully pointed out, no paying ore was ever discovered there. That was a rather disappointing start for a tour, but things picked up as the guide took us inside and showed us how miners bored holes, set charges, retrieved the ore, and sent it out of the mine. During the tour, three pieces of working machinery were activated using air pressure, and we certainly became aware of what the din inside a mine could be.

The tour took eighty minutes, including a tram ride from downtown Wallace. I felt that young children might become restless inside the mine, as we often stood in one spot, then another. I would not recommend the tour for those who are unsteady on their feet, as the terrain is uneven and occasionally wet.

Overall, the Sierra Silver Mine is worth touring, but it does not compare to Colorado's Old Hundred Mine (see page 105) near Silverton or the Mollie Kathleen (see page 66) north of Cripple Creek.

Wallace's Nine Mile Cemetery, north of town, features a convenient series of roads for exploring this lovely, large cemetery.

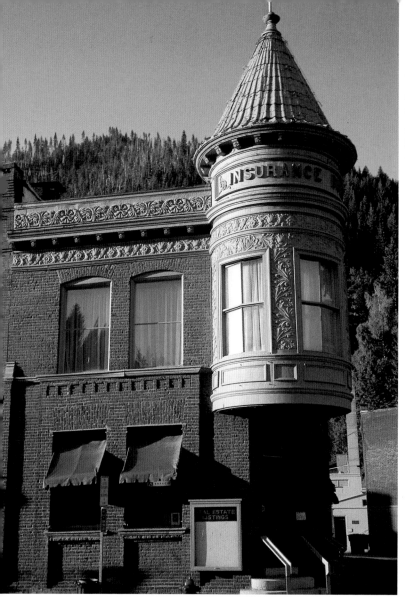

The pressed metal turret on the 1892 Rossi Insurance Building in Wallace is actually an architectural imitation of a turret across the street to the west.

it becomes Ninemile Creek Road. Where the one-mile marker appears on your right, look left for the entrance to the graveyard.

The Nine Mile Cemetery stands among pines along steep slopes. Narrow roads crisscross it, so you can survey it easily. It has hundreds of old markers partitioned into sections such as the Miners' Union, the Veterans, the Odd Fellows, the Eagles, the Grand Mound, the Forest Home, and the Catholic. The latter section, the farthest south, contains a monument to commemorate five men who died August 20, 1910, fighting the Big Blowup.

The Oasis Bordello Museum

I have been to three bordello museums: the Bird Cage Theater in Tombstone, Arizona; the Old Homestead in Cripple Creek, Colorado; and this one in Wallace, Idaho. The other two I would describe as "quaint," since the era of those brothels ended long ago.

The Oasis is very different, because it was in operation, incredibly, until 1988. The Oasis is not quaint. It is an unvarnished look at prostitution, and I found the look fascinating—but depressing. My guide's spiel was not at all lurid, but it was honest. The cheap paneling, the tiny rooms, the price list, the kitchen timers that were used to make sure patrons weren't staying overtime, the seven color-coded medicine cabinets in one bathroom—all that and more showed the tawdry, sad side of prostitution.

I must add, however, that it was unforgettable. Some people might find the entire experience offensive on moral grounds, but I did not. I certainly would not, however, have taken my daughter up those stairs when she was young, although my guide said many parents take their children through the tour.

The visit is not without humor: A band uniform hangs in the madam's quarters. According to my guide, the Wallace High School marching band was practicing its routines downtown in the morning, awakening the girls, who had been "off-duty" since only three o'clock in the morning. The madam made an offer: If the band would practice in the residential area instead, she would purchase new band uniforms. The offer was accepted. One of the uniform's colors, incidentally, is scarlet.

There is no admission to explore the main floor or the basement of the Oasis, neither of which was related to the brothel. The cost of visiting the upstairs, with its waiting room, cribs, madam's quarters, bathroom, and kitchen-dining area, is reasonable.

WHEN YOU GO

Wallace is 145 miles west of the Bearmouth exit, the route to Garnet. It is 114 miles west of Missoula, Montana, and 50 miles east of Coeur d'Alene, Idaho, on Interstate 90.

The concrete ore bin of Burke's Hecla Mine, at about six stories high, attests to the size of the mining operations north of Wallace, Idaho.

BURKE, IDAHO

Wallace (pages 216–223) shows little evidence of its mining past, except in museums and a mine tour. To get a better feel for that history, go up Canyon Creek to Burke.

Burke was one of several satellite towns of Wallace. Extensive lead and silver discoveries in 1884 led to the settling of a community so narrow that the town barely had room for streets. When the railroad arrived in 1888, things got even tighter: S. S. Glidden's Tiger Hotel had to be built over, rather than beside, Canyon Creek, with railroad tracks and the narrow main street running through the lobby. A later photograph (on display in the Wallace depot museum) shows a standard gauge steam locomotive competing with an automobile on the town's combination street and railroad right-of-way.

DRIVING TO AND AROUND BURKE, IDAHO

The same brochure (page 219) that guided you around Wallace also details the short trip from Wallace to Burke as you pass through the mostly vanished communities of Gem, Blackbear, Yellowdog, Cornwall, and Mace.

When you enter Burke today, you will pass several former company houses on your left. Up the road a bit, on your right, is the Hecla Mine's enormous concrete ore bin. This structure really gives a feel for the immensity of the Burke operations. Trains ran through the doors at the base of this behemoth, which looks about six stories tall, and the bins dropped ore into the empty cars. The ore was taken for processing at a mill down the canyon, followed by a trip to Smelterville, west of Wallace.

Next to the ore bin is the 1924 brick headquarters of the Hecla Mining Company. Behind it is the large brick Montana Power substation. Across the street stand several one-story, brick commercial buildings. Up the road .3 of a mile is a two-story brick building that served as the Hercules Mine's headquarters.

WHEN YOU GO

Burke is 7 miles north of Wallace on Idaho Highway 4, which is the last road on the east end of Wallace before entering the onramp to the interstate heading east.

225

7

UTAH

G H O S T S   O F

ZION

UTAH'S HISTORY IS FAR DIFFERENT FROM THE OTHER STATES in this book. In the others, settlers were encouraged, often even enticed, by the United States government to explore and tame the Western wilderness of the United States.

When Brigham Young brought his Latter-day Saints to the Great Salt Lake in 1847, he was intentionally leaving the United States—a country that had repeatedly persecuted the Mormons—for Mexico, whose land it was. His mission was to create a utopian society, called Zion, away from outside interference, and Mexican influence there was minimal. In fact, when the Mormons came to Utah, that was the very beginning of non-Indian settlements in the Great Basin of North America, which had previously been called the Great Desert, a fundamentally uninhabitable area.

One can imagine Brigham Young's consternation when his Zion became part of United States territory in July 1848, following the Mexican-American War. Would the religious freedom the Mormons sought be denied them yet again?

The end of the Mexican-American War resulted in the Mexican Cession, in which Mexico gave up what would eventually become the entire states of California, Utah, and Nevada, along with most of Arizona and parts of Colorado, New Mexico, and Wyoming.

In the Frisco Cemetery, Charles K. Odell's epitaph reads: "Farewell my wife and children all / From thee a father Christ doth call / Mourn not for me it is in vain / To call me to your side again." Note also the misspelling of "Poughkeepsie."

What Mexico ceded would soon yield the California Gold Rush, Nevada's Comstock Lode, and enormous deposits of copper in Arizona and Utah. The Mexican Cession eventually played an important role in America's becoming a world power.

In Zion, the settlers created a provisional state in 1849 called Deseret, a word meaning "honeybee" in the Book of Mormon. Deseret was never recognized by the United States, which created the Utah Territory in 1850. In February 1851, Brigham Young was chosen as the first governor of the territory, which included all of Utah, most of Nevada, and small portions of Wyoming and Colorado. Two months later, the State of Deseret dissolved itself and Utah became the operant name. (The word "Deseret" remains, however, as the name of a Mormon Church–affiliated newspaper, and it is symbolized by the hive of the honeybee on the Utah state emblem.)

Incidentally, the word "Utah" would seem to come from the Ute Indians. But there is no such word in their language. A tribal spokesman believes that "Utah" is an Anglicizing of what the Spanish called the Utes: *Yuta*, apparently meaning "Meat-Eaters."

Utahans repeatedly petitioned the federal government for statehood, all of which failed partially because of the Mormon practice of polygamy and also because of the fear that in Utah there would be no separation of church and state. In 1887, another attempt included a clause prohibiting polygamy, addressing one of the concerns. In the early 1890s, the Mormon People's Party was dissolved, with its members evenly joining the Republican and Democratic parties. With this final concern conveniently addressed for Republicans and Democrats in Washington, D.C., Utah achieved statehood in 1896.

In 1849, at the beginning of the California Gold Rush, Brigham Young told his followers that California was no place for Mormons, but he did encourage the mining of that which could be of practical use, like iron and coal. As a result, silver towns such as Silver Reef and Frisco had little Mormon influence, but the coal town of Scofield did.

The sequence of towns in this chapter begins with the northeasternmost site, Scofield, and travels through the heart of Utah to the southernmost, Grafton. The westernmost site, Frisco, leads you toward chapter 8, the ghost towns of Nevada.

IDAHO

WYOMING

84 15

Great Salt Lake

84 80

Salt Lake City

80

93A 80

40 189

15

Vernal

40 189

Utah Lake

189

Provo

40 40 191

Spanish Fork

Soldier Summit

6

0 25 Miles

0 25 Kilometers

89 96 191

Nephi

Fairview

SCOFIELD

6

Mt. Pleasant

Price

Delta

117

31

Green River

28

SPRING CITY

50

50

10

6 191

Salina

6 50

Green River

70

SAN FRANCISCO MOUNTAINS

15

70

70

COVE FORT

21

Milford

Colorado River

FRISCO

U T A H

191

Minersville

Beaver

21

15

Monticello

130

491

89

56

Cedar City

Lake Powell

Toquerville

Zion National Park

SILVER REEF

La Verkin

Leeds

9

Rockville

t. George

GRAFTON

Kanab

89

15

A R I Z O N A

COLORADO

SCOFIELD

Scofield has only a few ghostly buildings mixed in among more modern ones. It doesn't really have that "ghost town feeling." But if you are truly interested in being struck by the enormity of what tragedy can mean in a mining community, a visit to the Scofield Cemetery should be obligatory.

Coal deposits were found on the western slopes of Pleasant Valley around 1875. Two years later, the first commercial coal mine in Utah opened, with coal transported over mountain roads to towns in the Sanpete Valley. (If you take the road from Scofield to the next site in this book, Spring City (pages 234–239), you will follow one of the main routes.) When a vicious winter storm stranded miners in the mountains that first year, those who rode out the season had a new name for their camp: Winter Quarters.

A second camp, named for mining official Charles W. Scofield, was established out on the flat east of the narrow Winter Quarters Canyon, where there was more room to build.

To make the transportation of coal more profitable, a railroad was constructed from Springville, south of Provo, up Soldier Creek and over Soldier Summit. (If you came from Provo on U.S. Highway 6, you probably saw a coal train still traversing this same route.) The Utah & Pleasant Valley Railroad was begun in 1877 and completed to Scofield and Winter Quarters two years later.

The mining operations became a one-owner affair when the Utah Fuel Company purchased the mine. It in turn became a subsidiary in 1882 of one of the West's major railroads, the Denver & Rio Grande Western, which, naturally, consumed enormous quantities of coal. The mines of Pleasant Valley seemed assured of a long and profitable life, and, with its reputation as a safe operation, the Winter Quarters Mine became a sought-after employer for miners from around the United States and even Europe.

That reputation for safety came to a sudden end. A plaque attached to a monument just outside the Scofield Cemetery tells the tragic story: At 10:25 on the morning of May 1, 1900, a keg of powder at the Winter Quarters Mine No. 4 ignited, causing coal dust to rise and also ignite. Subsequent explosions of twenty-four kegs of black powder also included nearby Mine No. 1, killing a total of 200 miners (although some rescuers placed the total as high as 246), either from the explosions

Scofield's schoolhouse, the town's largest building, was erected in 1928, when the town was already in decline.

themselves or from suffocation in the resulting poisonous gas. Many others were injured in what was the nation's worst coal mining disaster at the time.

Miners who had escaped the blasts, joined by others from nearby mines, entered the shafts in a heroic effort to rescue those trapped inside, but mostly it became a mission to retrieve bodies, the last of which came out of the mine eleven days later. The disaster left 107 widows and 268 fatherless children.

The monument to the fallen Winter Quarters miners outside the cemetery features a touching bas-relief sculpture showing the anguished faces of miners, the mournful countenances of women and children, grave markers, and empty cabins—along with the names of the miners who died.

Winter Quarters and Scofield turned into mass morgues. The company board-inghouse at Winter Quarters was emptied to receive and identify the dead; the bodies were then taken to the schoolhouse for families to claim. The supply of 125 caskets in Salt Lake City was not sufficient, so a carload of 75 caskets from Denver was sent by train. Two large funerals were held in Scofield on May 5, a Lutheran one for the Finns killed and another for the Mormon dead. Three-quarters of the

This section of the Scofield Cemetery is dominated by the graves of coal miners who died in 1900 in what was then the country's worst mining disaster.

dead were buried in Scofield, while two funeral trains took the other fifty caskets for burial in various cemeteries in Utah and other states.

The mines reopened on May 28, but Winter Quarters and Scofield never fully recovered. As seams faltered, the coal was of a lower grade, and transportation costs made the mines unprofitable. They closed in 1928. Winter Quarters was a total ghost by 1930, and Scofield slowly died until after World War II, when it became a ghost as well. The population of Scofield in 2003 was twenty-six.

WALKING AND DRIVING AROUND SCOFIELD

Mining has made a mild resurgence in Scofield. When you drive to Spring City, the next entry in this book (pages 234–239), you will pass the huge Canyon Coal operation, with its lengthy conveyor belt, not far from Scofield.

Today, Scofield features mostly occupied buildings with perhaps a dozen dilapidated or empty structures. The dominant one is the stone and brick public schoolhouse, which stands on the west side of town on Church Street. It was erected in 1928, when Scofield, already in decline, must have looked toward a promising future that did not occur. Other empty structures include a mercantile and the Mountaineer Bar.

On the south end of town, along the highway, two informative signs chronicle the tragic history of Scofield and Winter Quarters. They feature a haunting photograph of the Luoma family, originally from Finland, who lost six sons and three grandsons in the Winter Quarters disaster, and a photo of a special train from Salt Lake City that carried the caskets of miners who were to be interred elsewhere.

The cemetery is across the railroad tracks on a hill on the east side of town. When you walk through the main gate, you immediately see a section of children's graves, reminding us that this is a place of more than one tragedy.

The miners buried in Scofield lie mostly in the northwest section of the cemetery. Their graves, even if they have an individual tombstone, are also delineated with a wooden marker. Also in the section is a special tomb for the unidentified victims. One elaborate, deteriorating monument is to those miners who were also members of the International Order of Odd Fellows.

I found one headstone particularly touching. It was for Robert and Llewelyn Williams, father and son, who died in the disaster. Robert was forty-five; his son did not reach his sixteenth birthday.

While I was walking around the cemetery, I watched four young girls, none likely older than ten, happily gathering some of the profusion of purple, white, yellow, and red wildflowers growing at the site. At this solemn place, I was glad to see such energy and happiness.

WHEN YOU GO

From Provo, head about 5 miles south on Interstate 15 to Spanish Fork. From there, take U.S. Highway 6 southeast for 37 miles to Soldier Summit. At about 5.5 miles beyond Soldier Summit, there is a turnoff onto Utah Highway 96. Scofield is 16.4 miles southwest of that junction.

SPRING CITY

Spring City is one of the historic treasures of Utah, but it is not a ghost town. I guarantee, however, that if you explore Spring City, a National Historic District, you will be as enchanted with it as I am and will be pleased it is in this book.

In the Latter-day Saint church, people certainly volunteer for various services to the church, but many are "called," which to Mormons means that God, through his prophet on Earth (the church President), has chosen a person for a certain duty. A "calling" is, then, a great honor. Such an honor occurred in 1852 when Brigham Young called James Allred of Manti to create a settlement at a location where springs had been used for years by Ute Indians and white scouts. A group of fifteen families built a fort around the most prominent spring and occupied it for a short time, calling it the Allred Settlement of Springtown. But widespread Ute hostilities began shortly after, and the fort and other dwellings were abandoned and subsequently burned by the Utes.

With Indian uprisings apparently over, Allred returned in 1859 with a second group of settlers, mostly Mormons from Denmark, who established farms in a community this time known as Spring Town and, informally, as Little Denmark. But the community was again abandoned in 1866, when Brigham Young ordered residents of smaller communities to find refuge

The home of Niels Borresen is made of rubble stone, not the more elegant limestone blocks of many of Spring City's homes. Built around 1864, the residence is one of the largest stone houses in the community.

The William and Margaret Osborne residence, made of polychrome brick, is one of the finer examples of Victorian architecture in this book. The home was later a hotel and now serves as a bed-and-breakfast inn.

in larger towns (in Spring Town's case, to Manti) because of renewed Ute conflicts known as the Black Hawk War.

Not to be confused with a better-known Black Hawk War that began in the Midwest in 1832, this war was the most serious conflict between settlers and Native Americans in Utah's history. It began with the seizing, and consuming, of Mormon farmers' cattle by starving Indians. A Ute war chief, Black Hawk, led a loose confederacy of desperate Utes, Paiutes, and Navajos against the settlers, resulting in the deaths of as many as seventy Mormons. Hundreds of Mormon militiamen retaliated by killing large numbers of Indians, including women and children. The conflicts didn't entirely end until two hundred federal troops, who had been repeatedly requested by church authorities starting eight years earlier, finally made their presence in 1872. The show of strength forced the Native Americans into submission.

Spring Town, however, was deemed safe to return to much earlier, in 1867. It became a permanent community, with more substantial buildings, including a church and a general store, and an increased population, reflected in the name change to Spring City in 1870. The town took on a more urbane look after the discovery of nearby oolite limestone deposits; as a result, quarried stone became the building material of choice.

In 1890, Spring City became a major shipping center for quarried stone, cream and cheese from its Danish farms, and general agricultural products when the Rio Grande Western Railway extended tracks across the Sanpete Valley. By 1900, Spring City was at its apex, with a population of more than twelve hundred. Although primarily Mormon, the town also had Methodist and Presbyterian churches.

The lure of larger cities began Spring City's slow deterioration, with the population decreasing every decade between the 1900s and the 1970s. The bypassing of Spring City by U.S. Highway 89 in 1957 contributed to this decline.

That decline actually helped save Spring City, because there was no need to destroy older structures to build new ones. When young families began to come to Spring City in the 1970s, they found lovely, solid buildings that could be restored, not obliterated. In each decade since the 1970s, the population has slowly increased, and additional historic buildings have been saved. In the 2000 census, 956 people resided in Spring City.

WALKING AND DRIVING AROUND SPRING CITY

Here is my cardinal rule for examining this wonderful town: You must drive every street and look carefully. Just when you think you're in a modern residential area, you'll see a century-old barn or outbuilding. Lovely historic homes are nestled among newer ones. A pioneer cemetery hides along a side street.

The structures of Spring City have a remarkable diversity. Many of the best are constructed of the locally quarried oolite limestone, but others are elegant brick, some are clapboard wood, some are adobe, while a few are hand-hewn log cabins. The varied architecture and building materials of Spring City make it one of the most interesting towns in the American West.

An outstanding booklet, "Spring City: A Guide to Architecture and History," is available at the Horseshoe Mountain Pottery and Gallery at 278 South Main. The problem is that the establishment, located in the 1905 Arthur Johnson Meat Market, is only open on Friday and Saturday afternoons. It is worth timing your visit so that you can acquire the booklet because it gives historical details, with color photographs, of seventy-four of Spring City's marvelous buildings, along with an accompanying map.

Naturally, I cannot include all those structures, so here are five favorites:

Main and Center streets, which intersect, form the core of Spring City. Two blocks south on Main at 200 South Street are excellent buildings on all four corners. On the northwest side stands the graceful, oolite limestone Latter-day Saint chapel, constructed between 1902 and 1911.

On the southwest corner is the 1894 brick William and Margaret Osborne House, now a bed-and-breakfast inn. With its elaborate eaves, shingled gables, and multicolored bricks, the Osborne House stands as one of the finest examples of Victorian architecture in this book.

The Hyde House is across the street from the Osborne home on the southeast corner of Main and 200 South. Built around 1868, the two-story, limestone building served as the official residence of Orson Hyde, one of the Mormon Church's twelve apostles, and Mary Ann Price Hyde, one of his eight wives.

On the northeast corner of the same intersection stands the Niels Borresen home, built around 1864. The two-foot-thick walls are made of rubble stone, not quarried blocks. Borresen, a native of Denmark, was a miller and a horticulturalist who had three wives. He was imprisoned twice for practicing polygamy.

The most dramatic building in town is the 1899 Spring City Public School, at 45 South 100 East. It was designed by the same architect as the Mormon chapel on Main, but they look nothing alike. The schoolhouse, like the Osborne home, features polychromatic masonry using locally fired bricks. The eight-classroom building is, at this writing, undergoing a complete restoration.

The Old Spring City Cemetery is on the east side of 100 East Street between 200 North and 300 North. Shaped like the state of Utah, the cemetery features headstones of Spring City's earliest settlers. Despite the lack of markers, a sign explains that the cemetery is filled with graves, many of them for children. A more modern graveyard is a mile west of Spring City on 300 North Street.

The Spring City Public School, built in 1899, has only eight classrooms despite its imposing size.

WHEN YOU GO

The route between Scofield and Spring City is one of the most beautiful drives in Utah. From Scofield, drive 2.7 miles south on Utah Highway 96 to the junction with Utah Highway 264. Take Highway 264 for 15.2 lovely miles up into the Wasatch Plateau until that highway meets Utah Highway 31. Take Highway 31 for 8.3 miles down to the Sanpete Valley and the town of Fairview, where there is a junction with U.S. Highway 89. From Fairview, head south 6 miles on U.S. 89 to Mount Pleasant. At the south end of town, Utah Highway 117 heads south for about 4 miles to Spring City.

COVE FORT

Cove Fort is the only remaining intact structure of the many fortresses built by the Mormons during the early years of settlement in the Utah Territory.

In 1849, Latter-day Saint President Brigham Young called Ira Hinckley to move from Coalville, north of present-day Park City, to Cove Creek, where he led a group of men to construct a stout fort to protect travelers and provide a waystation down the "Mormon Corridor," a series of roads, postal routes, and, eventually, telegraph stations that connected Mormon settlements from Idaho to Nevada.

The site was chosen because it was halfway between the towns of Fillmore and Beaver and because there was an existing wooden structure, Willden Fort, in which the working crews could find shelter and safety. There would, however, be no true town at Cove Creek because of its inadequate water supply.

In a mere eleven months, Hinckley and his crew assembled a formidable fortress. Built of lava stone and a dark limestone available nearby, the fort is one hundred feet square and eighteen feet high, with walls four feet thick at the footings and two-and-a-half feet at the top. Massive wooden doors were placed at the east and west ends with sand filling the gap between the inside and outside planks to blunt bullets and keep flaming arrows from burning the doors.

The interior featured twelve rooms, six each on the north and south walls, all six interconnected. The northern rooms were living room-bedrooms, each with its own fireplace, while the southern ones were working rooms, including a post office, a kitchen, an assembly room, a weaving area, a stagecoach office, and, later, a telegraph station.

Between 1867 and about 1890, Cove Fort served an invaluable purpose, connecting communities through the telegraph, mail service, and two daily stages, one coming north and one coming south. A blacksmith lived on the premises, with his shop outside the western walls. On occasion, as many as seventy people were housed and fed within the fort. There was never an assault on the structure, likely because its intimidating stature discouraged hostilities. There were, however, many Indian attacks on Mormon farmers, especially between 1866 and 1868 (see the Spring City and Grafton entries, pages 234–239 and 244–249).

By the turn of the twentieth century, Cove Fort had outlived its purpose, and the church sold it to the Otto Keslar family. In 1988, the Hinckley family

Although no attack was ever made on Cove Fort, likely because of its imposing appearance, Indian hostilities did occur in the vicinity.

purchased the fort from the Keslars and presented it to the church. A completely restored fort was dedicated in 1994, with historic furniture, artifacts, and implements reflecting the period of 1867 to 1877. In addition, the original Ira Hinckley cabin from Coalville was also moved to the site.

TOURING COVE FORT

The only way to see the inside of Cove Fort, which is listed on the National Register of Historic Places, is to take a tour accompanied by a guide from the Church of Jesus Christ of Latter-day Saints. There is no admission charge. My guide, who was pleasant and informative and who in no way pressured his beliefs upon me, led me from room to room, on a couple of occasions handing me off to a second guide who had a thorough knowledge of certain rooms.

I was inside Cove Fort for about thirty-five minutes, which might have been longer than some people, because I asked many questions about life at the fort.

Note: Some people might be uncomfortable in what is at least, in part, a Mormon proselytizing effort, as you will be offered various books and videos at the end of your tour. I, however, felt no such discomfort.

WHEN YOU GO

From Spring City, drive 70 miles south on U.S. Highway 89 to its junction with Interstate 70 just south of Salina. From there, take Interstate 70 southwest for 56 miles to its terminus with Interstate 15.

Cove Fort is just north of the junction of Interstates 15 and 70. Signs clearly mark the turnoffs from both interstates.

SILVER REEF

Silver Reef is not the important ghost town it once was. It has been absorbed into a suburban setting and has lost the abandoned look it had when I first saw it decades ago. It is nevertheless included in this book for two reasons: It was a vital, historic mining center in southern Utah, and it is close enough to wonderful Grafton (see following entry, pages 244–249) that you might as well take a look while you're in the area.

Silver Reef stands as a testament that not all common knowledge is correct. Virtually all prospectors, mining experts, assayers, and metallurgists once knew that sandstone simply does not contain silver. However, prospector John Kemple proved in 1866 that the common knowledge was wrong. In a white sandstone reef south of what is now Silver Reef, he found a significant amount of silver. He nevertheless went off to Nevada, but he returned to Utah in 1870 and developed the Harrisburg Mining District.

Another prospector, William Tecumseh Barbee, also discovered silver in sandstone in 1874. Grubstaked by two Salt Lake City banking brothers, Barbee founded the Tecumseh Mine and other claims. The brothers, believing the "experts" who proclaimed sandstone's inability to hold silver, backed out of the investment but allowed Barbee to keep the claims. His subsequent strike gave rise to Bonanza City. Land was expensive in the new town, so newcomers set up a tent city nearby and called it the Rockpile. When a rush to the area ensued, the Rockpile became Silver Reef, which soon absorbed Bonanza City.

Silver Reef, which eventually had a population between fifteen hundred and two thousand, featured such enterprises as saloons, mercantiles, drugstores, gambling houses, a bank, and a Wells Fargo Express Company office. It also could boast of such civic refinements as a Catholic church with a small hospital in its basement, fraternal lodges, a school, and a racetrack. Because it was a silver mining town, Silver Reef was largely non-Mormon, although citizens purchased Mormon goods and many of the town's buildings were erected using Latter-day Saint labor. The fact that the town's racetrack was the center of the action on Sunday proves that Silver Reef was not under Latter-day Saint restrictions.

The glory years of Silver Reef lasted only from 1878 until 1882. The price of silver dropped by almost half in 1881 at the same time that area mines began to give out

The stout Wells Fargo office in Silver Reef is reminiscent of similar buildings in California's Gold Rush Country.

and to flood. By 1884, the town was emptying, and the major mines and mills ceased production by 1891. Although some mining continued on a small scale, Silver Reef was essentially dead, but not before producing twenty-five million dollars in ore.

WALKING AND DRIVING AROUND SILVER REEF

The parking area for Silver Reef is adjacent to its most prominent building, the 1878 Wells Fargo office, listed on the National Register of Historic Places. It was restored in 1991 and now serves as a combination art gallery and history museum. The gallery features Western art, and the museum offers historical photographs, arrowheads, pottery shards, miners' tools, and other artifacts.

Across the street to the south is the 1876 former John Rice bank, now a private residence. North of the gallery/museum is a reconstruction of the Cosmopolitan Restaurant and several walls of former Silver Reef businesses. Beyond the townsite to the north is the rather surreal sight of suburban homes winding up a hill. Behind the town to the west is considerable evidence of Silver Reef's mining past: a wooden hopper, mining debris, and the stone retaining walls and foundations of the Barbee and Walker Mill.

Silver Reef's two cemeteries, Protestant and Catholic, are back toward the interstate. Retrace your route one mile from the Wells Fargo building, where a sign will direct you to the cemeteries immediately ahead. You'll also notice a mine's headframe on the hill southeast of the graveyards.

WHEN YOU GO

From Cove Fort, drive 111 miles south on Interstate 15 to the Leeds North Exit, Exit 23. Silver Reef is 1.4 miles west of that exit. Prominent signs lead you to the townsite.

GRAFTON

As mentioned earlier in this chapter, Mormon Church President Brigham Young sent out pioneers in all directions from Salt Lake City to claim territory by settling in desirable locations for agriculture.

One crop he believed would help the Mormons achieve self-sufficiency was cotton. He sent settlers to what would become Santa Clara, a community west of present-day St. George, to plant cotton in 1854.

The experiment was a success, which caused Young to send out more settlers to do the same. The cotton-producing area of southern Utah became known as Dixie as a nod to the American South. One of Dixie's cotton settlements, begun in 1859, was Grafton, a community established on the south side of the Virgin River and reportedly named after Grafton, Massachusetts.

Two years later, the Civil War made cotton a more precious commodity outside of the Confederacy, and Young's foresight made him look like the prophet the Mormons believe he was.

But you can't eat cotton, and originally the Grafton farmers overplanted the crop in lieu of others and had trouble feeding their families. From then on, cotton production was secondary to corn and other staples, including fruit orchards.

A Virgin River flood in 1862 that destroyed their townsite caused Grafton residents to relocate a mile upstream, on higher ground, the present location of Grafton today. Despite frequent battles with the unpredictable river (irrigation ditches were constantly being destroyed, filled with sand, and rerouted), the small community of fewer than two hundred prospered.

The town was abandoned temporarily between 1866 and 1868 when hostilities with Ute Indians caused Brigham Young to order a consolidation of villages for mutual protection. During that time, Grafton residents tended their crops by day and retreated at night. At least three graves in the Grafton Cemetery attest to the dangers of that time. When hostilities ceased, Grafton returned to its former life.

In 1906, many Grafton farmers assisted in the digging of the Hurricane Canal, which promised a more reliable and predictable source of irrigation water for agriculture. They also were digging the grave of Grafton, because most families moved to the new area, about twenty miles downstream from the townsite. Grafton slowly became a ghost town. The last residents to leave were the son and

Hollywood has used Grafton at least a half-dozen times because of its lovely buildings and remarkable backdrop of Zion National Park. On the left is the town's combination chapel and school; on the right is the home of Alonzo and Nancy Russell.

The headstones of the Grafton Cemetery blend in seamlessly with their surroundings. Several of the dead in the graveyard died from Indian attacks.

daughter-in-law of Alonzo Russell, who lived in his father's house from 1917 until they moved to St. George in 1944.

But Grafton was not a completely forgotten ghost town. Hollywood has featured the picturesque spot several times, most notably in the 1969 film classic *Butch Cassidy and the Sundance Kid*.

WALKING AND DRIVING AROUND GRAFTON

You will pass the Grafton Cemetery as you approach the townsite. I suggest that you first go to the townsite and, when you have explored it, return to the cemetery, because you will then be able to attach more importance to at least two graves.

As you enter Grafton, listed on the National Register of Historic Places, you'll pass a wooden barn and the 1877 brick home of John and Ellen Wood. Beyond that house is a parking area in front of one of the most picturesque ghost town sights in the American West: Grafton's 1886 adobe schoolhouse and the 1862 Alonzo and Nancy Russell home, also made of adobe, both constructed with bricks crafted on the site. Behind the buildings rise the stunning red cliffs of Mount Kinesava in Zion National Park. Across an open area from the Russell home stands the 1879 hand-hewn wood cabin of Louisa Maria Foster Russell, who was Alonzo Russell's third wife. She and her six children lived in the home directly across from Alonzo and his first wife, Nancy. (I have read no mention of his second wife.)

The schoolhouse, which also served as a church meetinghouse and community center, has a foundation of lava rocks quarried nearby and features beams that were brought more than seventy-five miles to this site from Mount Trumbull in northern Arizona. The building last had students in 1919. The schoolhouse has been saved from deterioration and vandalism by a complete restoration, finished in 2000.

The two-story Alonzo Russell house exterior was restored in 2004; an interior restoration is planned.

The Grafton Cemetery contains, according to a sign at the site, between seventy-four and eighty-four graves. In addition to the original settlers, that includes some Southern Paiute Indians, who assisted the early residents.

The cemetery features the graves of Alonzo Russell (1821 to 1910) and his first wife, Nancy (1825 to 1903), who is remembered on her epitaph as "a kind and affectionate wife, fond mother, and a friend to all." His third wife, Louisa, who

Grafton's John and Ellen Wood residence is on private property. It and a neighboring barn have been stabilized by the owners.

was thirteen years younger than Nancy and who outlived Alonzo by seven years, is buried on the other side of Alonzo.

Other markers attest to the violence of frontier life. According to their headstones, Robert M. Berry, his wife Mary Isabelle, and his brother Joseph were killed on the same day in 1866 by Navajo raiders. They were not Grafton residents, nor were they killed there, but their bodies were brought to this cemetery because Grafton was the county seat at that time. They were attempting to reach their home in Glendale, a now-vanished town near present-day Colorado City, Arizona.

The year 1866 was particularly difficult for settlers: In less than four months, eleven people died in the small community because of diphtheria, scarlet fever, or murder by Indians. In addition, two young girls, Loretta Russell (age fourteen) and Elizabeth Woodbury (age thirteen), died in a "swing accident." This last seems unnecessarily tragic and makes one wonder about the circumstances; playing on a swing shouldn't, after all, be fatal.

WHEN YOU GO

From Silver Reef, return to Interstate 15 and drive 3.6 miles north to Exit 27, for Toquerville, and head southeast on Utah Highway 17 for 6 miles to La Verkin. From there, take Utah Highway 9 southeast for 15 miles to Rockville.

In Rockville, a sign on the east side of town directs you to Grafton, 3.4 miles away. That sign is on Bridge Road, the only street in Rockville that crosses the Virgin River. Not long after traversing the 1924 steel truss bridge, you'll turn west as Bridge Road becomes Grafton Road. The route turns to dirt in 2.2 miles from Rockville, which in dry weather should be fine for a passenger car. The left turnoff to the cemetery is .9 of a mile from the road's turning to dirt, and the townsite is .3 of a mile to the right, toward the river, beyond that turnoff.

FRISCO

Frisco is what the devoted ghost-towner seeks. It sits in the middle of nowhere, its population is zero, and it features several ruins, a forlorn cemetery, and five beehive charcoal kilns.

When rich horn silver was found at the foot of San Francisco Mountain in 1876, the mining camp of Frisco came into being adjacent to the aptly named Horn Silver Mine. Frisco, which had a peak population of about four thousand, was entirely dependent upon shipping for its existence. Everything, even water, had to be hauled to the remote desert town, originally by mule trains and later by the Utah Southern Railroad, which was extended to Frisco in 1880.

The scarcity of water apparently required alternative means to slake thirst, as more than twenty saloons operated in what became known as one of the wildest towns in the West. One wag described it as "Dodge City, Tombstone, Sodom, and Gomorrah all rolled into one." A tough-minded marshal hired from Pioche, Nevada, was brought in. He reportedly killed six outlaws on his first day on the job. That seemed to encourage other members of the criminal element to depart, and Frisco calmed down.

When day-shift workers reported for duty at the Horn Silver Mine in February 1885, they were told to stay outside because of tremors in the ground. The night shift came to the surface, and within minutes, a huge cave-in occurred with such a jolt that it was felt in Milford, almost fifteen miles away. The timing was amazing: No one was even injured. The mine returned to production within the year but never at the level it had formerly achieved. Prior to the collapse, more than sixty million dollars in silver, gold, copper, lead, and zinc had been extracted from the mines in less than ten years. In the next thirty years, it produced only twenty million more.

Frisco declined steadily after the cave-in, and, by the turn of the twentieth century, the town had a mere handful of businesses and a population of a few hundred. It was a complete ghost by the 1920s.

WALKING AND DRIVING AROUND FRISCO

As you head west from Milford, you'll come to the Frisco Summit. It's easy to miss the ruins of Frisco .4 of a mile beyond the summit to your right, because they're back over your shoulder as the highway turns (see "When You Go," below). When you enter the townsite, at this writing you'll find large iron vats, a wooden building still under roof, numerous rock walls and foundations, mining debris such as an old boiler, and a water tank fallen on its side. That would suffice for most ghost town purists, but the best remnants are standing on a western hill: five stone beehive charcoal kilns, used to turn wood into charcoal to feed smelters (for a more detailed explanation, see the Piedmont, Wyoming, entry, pages 136–139). Of the five kilns, three are virtually intact.

On my last visit, a protective chain-link fence around the kilns had been breached. That allowed me to photograph the kilns more effectively, but the fence needs to be repaired, as there is evidence of vandalism.

The cemetery, southwest of the townsite, features some excellent headstones. One, for Boswell W. Hopkins (1852 to 1879), has the Latin inscription from Horace, *Non Omnis Moriar* ("Not All of Me Shall Die"). Another, for Tommy James, who died at ten months in 1883, bears the epitaph "Whose all of life's a rosy ray / Blushed into dawn and passed away."

WHEN YOU GO

From Grafton, retrace your route to Exit 27 on Interstate 15. Drive northeast for 39 miles, just north of Cedar City, to Exit 62. Proceed north on Utah Highway 130 for 37 miles to Minersville. From there, take Utah Highway 21 for 13 miles to Milford.

From the intersection of West Center Street and Main Street (where Utah Highways 21 and 257 split) in Milford, go west on Highway 21 for 14.2 miles. There a turnoff heads north into the Frisco townsite. If you miss that turnoff, do not go beyond the historical marker on the right side of the highway, which is .2 of a mile past the turnoff. From there, you can backtrack to the turnoff and head in to the townsite, which will then be clearly visible. Or, heading west from that marker, you can take the southern of two roads (the northern is an old railroad bed that takes you to the locked gate of the Horn Silver Mine) for .5 of a mile to the fenced Frisco Cemetery.

Frisco is an abandoned site, one that should be on every ghost town enthusiast's "must see" list. The town's ruins stand beyond these charcoal kilns.

8
NEVADA
GHOSTS OF THE
SILVER STATE

WHEN GOLD AND THEN SILVER WERE FOUND in the Utah Territory in the late 1850s, many California argonauts rushed to the area, especially when word of the Comstock Lode's enormous quantities of silver reached their state. The newcomers, however, did not want to be part of a territory that was governed by Mormon leader Brigham Young. (For more, see the introduction to chapter 7, page 227–228.) People in the Carson Valley formed their own territorial government, which they had no right to do, because the recognized government resided in Salt Lake City.

Two years later, however, the U.S. Congress effectively legitimized the Carson Valley dissidents, creating the Nevada Territory by essentially cutting the Utah Territory in half. (Nevada, incidentally, means "snow-covered" or "snow-capped," as in the Sierra Nevada mountain range.) The territory was then rushed into statehood in 1864, just before that year's national election, because Abraham Lincoln needed more votes for the Thirteenth Amendment (abolishing slavery) and because the Union needed another state to support Lincoln to demonstrate to the Confederacy that the Union was strong. Lincoln signed the statehood proclamation even though Nevada did not have the sixty

The Gold Dust Saloon in Gold Point was built in 1908, when the metal of choice in the town's mines was horn silver, not gold.

thousand citizens required for statehood. Patriotism was running high in the new state, and citizens wanted to do what they could to support the United States. Hence their state motto: "All For Our Country."

The best ghost towns in Nevada demonstrate the wide variety of sites in the Mountain West. Austin is a semighost, with many commercial businesses in disrepair and disuse. Two of its three lovely churches do not hold services. Its old schoolhouse is vacant.

Belmont is more of a true ghost, off the power grid and with no gas station, no restaurants, and only one place for lodging. It also has some of the loveliest and most picturesque remnants in this book.

Goldfield is an excellent example of the boom-and-bust cycle of ghost towns. It features an enormous but vacant hotel, an elaborate but crumbling high school, and an imposing for-tresslike courthouse. But Goldfield is barely hanging on, its railroad long gone and its future not promising.

Gold Point is the best surviving mining camp in the West that is not protected as a state park. It has about three dozen wood-frame structures, including false-front commercial build-ings and miners' shacks. Most towns like it have long since disappeared because of neglect, weather, and vandalism. Gold Point is a rare treasure.

Rhyolite is a reminder that permanence is relative. Except for its glorious depot and its unusual bottle house, Rhyolite shows only photogenic skeletons of its glory days.

Berlin, like Gold Point, is a wood-frame mining camp, but it is protected as part of a Nevada State Park.

Virginia City, the final entry in this book's six-state canvass of ghost towns, features some of the finest buildings of the frontier West: extravagant mansions, a dramatic church, impres-sive civic buildings, huge mining structures, and a commercial district of wood-frame and brick edifices unrivaled in this book. Add in a steam train ride, multiple museums, mine and mill tours, gaming-house saloons, restaurants, and busy shops, and Virginia City becomes a vibrant combi-nation of a former mining bonanza and a present-day tourist mecca.

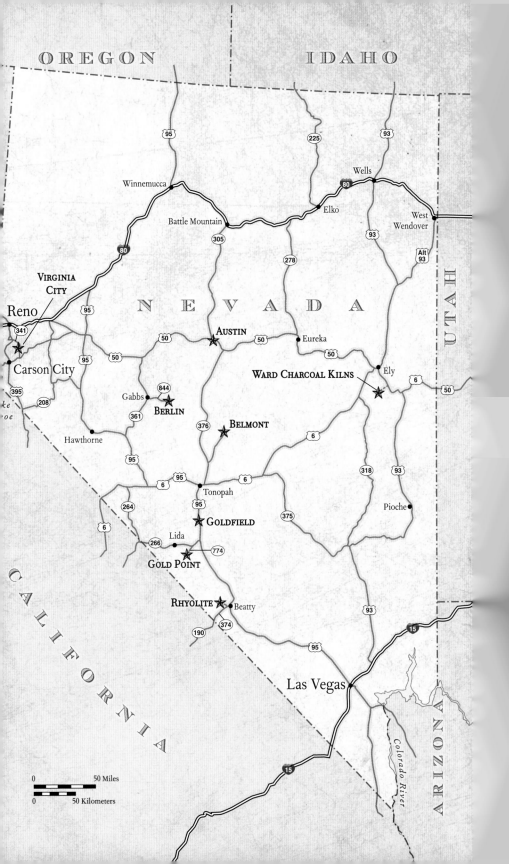

THE WARD CHARCOAL KILNS

NEVADA

Silver ore was discovered in 1872 in Ward Gulch, and the resulting town of Ward had a population of about fifteen hundred by 1877 and featured two smelters and a twenty-stamp mill. The town was dead by the late 1880s except for sporadic mining attempts in 1906, the late 1930s, and even in the 1960s. Little remains at the site except for foundations and a small cemetery.

You want to visit the Ward area today for the outstanding charcoal kilns, three miles south of the townsite, which were constructed around 1876. The kilns stand thirty feet high, with a diameter of twenty-seven feet. During the operation of these kilns, the vicinity was completely denuded of timber for a radius of about thirty-five miles. (For an explanation of the wood-to-charcoal kiln process, see the Piedmont, Wyoming, entry, page 136–139.)

The Ward Charcoal Kilns, southeast of Ely, are some of the finest-made, best-preserved kilns in the American West.

The kilns provided charcoal for Ward furnaces to smelt the lead ore. When a railroad reached Ward in the early 1880s, it eventually brought in coke, made from coal by a similar process, which put the Ward charcoal kilns out of business.

These kilns are highlighted in this book—even though they are not near a featured ghost town—because of their preservation. They are much more complete than the ones at Piedmont, Wyoming; Nicholia or Bayhorse, Idaho; or Frisco, Utah. They are also more beautiful. The craftsmanship of the Italian makers of these kilns, with their elegant stone entrances, makes them the best charcoal kilns I have ever seen—and I've seen hundreds.

WHEN YOU GO

If you are coming from Frisco, Utah, the final entry in chapter 7, drive 80 miles northwest on Utah Highway 21 to a junction with U.S. Highway 50 and U.S. Highway 6 just northwest of Baker, Nevada. From that junction, follow U.S. 50 and U.S. 6 for 45 miles to the marked turnoff for the Ward Charcoal Ovens State Historic Park. (These kilns are called "ovens" in this state park, even though that term is usually used for coal-to-coke structures.)

If you are coming from Ely, the turnoff to the kilns is 12.2 miles southeast of Ely's junction of U.S. 50, U.S. 6, and U.S. Highway 93. (An earlier turnoff to the site takes you down a long washboard road; I'd advise going beyond that turnoff and taking the much smoother route in.) From that second turnoff, the kilns are 6.4 miles down a very good road, with signs clearly posted.

AUSTIN

Austin is one of three major towns along a stretch of U.S. Highway 50, a route widely known as the Loneliest Road in America. Ely, the farthest east of the three, features many turn-of-the-twentieth-century buildings, a scenic train ride, and a railroad museum. West of Ely seventy-five miles is Eureka, which contains several photogenic buildings in a living town. Although those communities are historic and interesting, Austin, sixty-eight miles west of Eureka, is the only one with that elusive "ghost town feeling."

One of the last frontiers of the American West, at least in its contiguous states, was the "Great Desert," an area roughly extending from the Great Salt Lake to the eastern slopes of the Sierra Nevada. It was inhabited by nomadic Indians and traversed principally by Pony Express riders, the Overland Stage, and emigrants heading west.

Along the Pony Express and Overland Stage route stood a stop called Jacob's Spring, near the intermittently running Reese River. In 1862, apparently in search of a missing horse, William Talcott found a promising quartz-laden vein. The spot became known as Pony Canyon, and within a few months, the word was out: "Ho! For the Reese River!"

Within a year of the first discovery, Pony Canyon became a silver mecca, with freight teams, stages, and stragglers heading east from Virginia City. At the base of Pony Canyon grew the camp of Clifton, while in the canyon itself was the fledgling camp of Austin, reportedly named for Austin, Texas. Originally, Clifton was the location of choice because it was on flat ground. But the silver mines were in the canyon, and when better roads were constructed up to an area widened to allow for more buildings, Clifton became merely a staging area for shipment to Austin, which was a burgeoning city of about seven thousand people and, in the summer of 1863, the newly crowned seat of Lander County.

Austin is located on the western edge of the Toiyabe Range, and as prospectors fanned out all through the mountains, the town became the supply center for the entire area. Incorporated in 1864, Austin eventually featured banks, hotels, gaslights along the city streets, lovely churches, and a daily newspaper: the *Reese River Reveille*. The Manhattan Silver Company brought a steadying element to

St. George's Episcopal Church in Austin is the only historic church in town that still has regular Sunday services.

the town in 1865 when it consolidated mining properties and erected a mill. Solid production of silver ore fueled a prosperity that lasted throughout the 1870s.

Traveling journalist J. Ross Browne complimented Austinites by saying, "The population is one of the best I have seen in a mining town—active, industrious, hospitable, and orderly." Of Austin's location, however, he added, " I know of no reason at all why any human being should live in such a country; and yet some people do, and they seem to like it."

In 1880, the Nevada Central Railroad connected Austin to the Transcontinental Railroad at Battle Mountain, giving rise to even more optimism about Austin, because it meant shipping costs would markedly decrease. The line ended below Pony Canyon at what used to be Clifton, and a spur line, the Austin City Railway, took goods from the Nevada Central up to Austin. It was known as the Mule's Relief because goods could be sent uphill by rail rather than by pack animals.

By the time the Nevada Central arrived, however, the peak years for the Reese River District were already over. Mining gradually slowed until 1887, when operations ceased altogether, after producing more than nineteen million dollars in silver. They were revived by Anson Phelps Stokes for a decade commencing in 1894. (On your driving tour of town, you will see Stokes' primary legacy in Austin.) Modest mining efforts in the twentieth century brought continued hopes, all of which eventually faded.

WALKING AND DRIVING AROUND AUSTIN

Austin features eleven buildings or sites on the National Register of Historic Places. You will see the first as you enter Austin from the east—a small, one-story, granite building on the north side of the highway. This is the 1863 Gridley Store, owned by grocer Ruel C. Gridley. As a consequence of losing an election bet in April 1864, Gridley had to carry a fifty-pound sack of flour through town while jovially heckled by townspeople. In a subsequent celebration for the completion of his "penance," Gridley offered to auction off his flour sack to the highest bidder, with the proceeds donated to the U.S. Sanitary Commission, a charity aiding ill

At the first service at Austin's St. Augustine's Catholic Church, erected in 1866, tickets were sold to the mass to help pay for the church's new roof.

Leland House, now a private residence, served as a boardinghouse and restaurant in the 1880s.

or wounded Union soldiers. The public-spirited citizens then proceeded to buy, re-auction, and re-buy the sack repeatedly until the total raised for the charity, in that day alone, was about $6,000. Furthermore, Gridley still had the sack.

Gridley's flour sack became a symbol of patriotic generosity, both in Nevada and all across the nation, and when Gridley sold his then-famous sack for the final time in 1865 at the Sanitary Fair in St. Louis, one estimate says he had raised an astonishing $275,000 for the charity, which was the forerunner of the Red Cross.

Main Street has a downhill run from the Gridley Store all the way through town. Fermin Bruner, who spent his childhood years in Berlin (see page 290–291) and then Austin after the turn of the twentieth century, remembered riding a large bobsled packed with children, with a coal oil lamp on the front, down a snow-packed Main Street. By that time, Austin's heyday was over, and he reported that there was little horse and buggy traffic to worry about.

The Austin Museum, on your left at 180 Main Street as you head into town, is a good place to start your exploration. It features five rooms of displays and many historic photographs.

West of the museum is the Toiyabe Cafe, which, in addition to good food when I ate there, has an invaluable brochure featuring a walking or driving tour. The tour even suggests a route to follow, beginning back at Gridley's Store.

Since you should have that brochure, I won't detail it here but rather point out some of my favorite Austin buildings.

Down Main Street from the café is St. George's Episcopal Church, also on the National Register of Historic Places. Built of locally fired brick, the church has a lovely, original interior featuring a handsome Mills organ, which was brought around Cape Horn for installation in the then-new church in 1878. The church is still in active use, and, on Sundays, Austinites expect to hear the tolling of the church's bell.

Two other attractive brick churches, also on the historic register, are on Court Street, one block north of Main. The more dramatic is St. Augustine's Catholic Church, built in 1866 and the oldest Catholic church still standing in Nevada. Nearby is the more austere Methodist church, constructed in the same year.

Down Main Street west of the Episcopal church stands the 1871 former Lander County Courthouse. If it's open, go up to the second floor to see the original courtroom. A judge told me that the jurors' swivel chairs have surprised many occupants because of how far back they sway. The county seat was moved to Battle Mountain in 1979, but the building still serves county purposes.

Although the tour brochure does not feature any residences, there are several to view on your tour of Austin. Across the street from the courthouse is my favorite, a wonderfully restored private residence called Leland House, which was built of adobe in the 1860s, with later brick additions in the rear. The original roof consisted of more than two thousand flattened tin cans, their ends carefully crimped together. It was a boardinghouse, but it also offered meals to the public, under both Maggie Eames, who purchased the building in the 1860s, and Cynthia

Leland, who bought it in 1884. The latter placed a large sign on the roof proclaiming it "Leland House." An advertisement that year in the *Reveille* boasted, "The table is supplied at all times with the best the market affords. Delicacies in season. Board . . . $1.00 Single Meals . . . 50¢."

Some of the historic buildings in the main business district have been so altered that they have lost their historic appearance. A notable exception is the International Hotel, originally constructed in 1859 in Virginia City. When it was taken down in 1863, to be replaced by a larger, more elaborate hotel in that location, portions of the original were packed onto freight wagons and shipped to Austin. Now a café and saloon, it features a marvelous bar with an elaborate, mirrored back, which, like the Episcopal church's organ, was also brought around Cape Horn.

Stokes Castle is Austin's most famous landmark, and that is truly unfortunate, because many structures are far more attractive and have more history—but Stokes Castle remains Austin's oddity. It was apparently fashioned, according to a Nevada historical sign at the site, after a tower near Rome. Begun in 1896 and completed a year later, what is now called Stokes Castle—but was always called The Tower by its creator—is a three-story monstrosity made of local granite. The tower was the inspiration, if that's the right word, of Anson Phelps Stokes, a railroad and mining tycoon with prominent blueblood Eastern roots. If I sound a bit harsh about this building, I must add that I have seen photos of it in its heyday, and it is hard to imagine that the monolith was ever, in anybody's eyes, even remotely attractive. But famous it remains. It was momentarily occupied by Stokes' family in 1897. Despite its sumptuous furnishings at the time, one can almost hear a collective "Oh, dear!" from the visiting family when they first saw it. Despite that, it is on the National Register of Historic Places. To see Stokes' abomination, take Castle Road, on the west end of Austin, southwest for .6 of a mile.

West of Castle Road and down the hill on U.S. 50 is the beautiful Austin Cemetery, one of the more interesting graveyards in this book. With sections for Catholics, Masons, Odd Fellows, and ordinary citizens, it contains a generous collection of markers of varied materials and several ornate fences. One elaborate headstone is of an angel, reading from a book, for Mrs. L. W. Compton, a native of County Limerick, Ireland, who died in 1900 at the age of fifty-six. What seems a bit arrogant to me is that Mr. L. W. Compton did not see fit to have his wife's first name on the stone.

Austin seems like a rather small town now, but the size of its cemetery attests to the large population that once lived there. The graveyard is divided into four sections.

The road on the east end of the cemetery heads down a hill and into the rodeo grounds. This was the site of Clifton, the rival to Austin that disappeared. It was here that the Nevada Central Railroad had its terminus, and a plaque marks the location of the railroad's roundhouse and turntable. Fermin Bruner, the same little boy who bobsledded through town, said that the highlight of his day was when the train crew would allow him and the other boys to help push the manual turntable, with a locomotive aboard, in order to back the engine into its shed for the night. (The railroad was abandoned in 1938.)

WHEN YOU GO

Austin is 143 miles west of Ely and 168 miles east of Reno on U.S. Highway 50.

BELMONT

Silver reportedly discovered by an Indian in late 1865 caused a rush to the Toquima Range, with eager prospectors abandoning their workings in Austin, Ione, and other Nevada camps. The town that formed near the diggings was called Belmont, apparently for another town elsewhere in the United States. This Belmont first appeared in print in Austin's newspaper, the *Reese River Reveille* in June 1866, and in February of the following year, the same newspaper crowed, "the excitement . . . appears to be unabated, and the influx of strangers continues, and many a traveler is lucky if he finds a place to lay his head under shelter."

Later that same year, Belmont's own *Silver Bend Reporter* featured advertisements for an array of enterprises, including mercantiles, saloons, a drugstore, restaurants, hotels, a brewery, a bank, a dentist's office, and the Austin & Belmont Stage Company. A ten-stamp mill processed silver ore, and five sawmills provided lumber from the native pine and cedar.

Belmont's former Nye County Courthouse was completed in 1876, at about the same time that the area's silver deposits depleted. Belmont lost the county seat in 1905 to Tonopah.

Belmont took the seat of Nye County from Ione in 1867 when its population grew to two thousand citizens. It became the hub of commerce for a radius of almost a hundred miles, but it remained isolated, with goods coming by rail from San Francisco and Sacramento to Austin, where they were then shipped by pack train ninety miles to Belmont. East of town, the open flats and numerous springs brought farmers and ranchers to Monitor Valley.

The bonanza years, as was often the case in mining towns, were short. Only ten years after the discovery of silver, the mines began to play out, even as an elegant, brick, two-story courthouse was completed. Minor discoveries kept Belmont in business into the 1880s, but the population declined to less than two hundred, with many of those employed by Nye County for governing duties.

When Tonopah became a rising mining star beginning in 1900, Belmont's days were numbered. The county seat was moved to Tonopah in 1905, and Belmont lost its post office six years later. Sporadic mining and reworking of old mill tailings kept a few people in town, but by the end of World War I, Belmont was a ghost.

WALKING AND DRIVING AROUND BELMONT

As you enter downtown Belmont from the south, you'll see a series of ruins on either side of the street. The brick remnant on your left was the First National Bank, followed by a series of slate walls of other businesses. On the opposite side once stood a restaurant, the two-story Cosmopolitan Saloon, a market, two hardware stores, a saloon, and a mercantile. At the end of the street stands the former Combination Mining Company building, now a delightful bed-and-breakfast inn.

The two-story brick courthouse, one of the more photographed historic buildings in Nevada, stands on a knoll west of town. Tours are offered occasionally. The interior, at this writing, is largely vacant, but the building is structurally sound, due to recent foundation, roof, and exterior refurbishment. Carved into one of the first-floor doorframes is the name of Charles Manson, who, with his "family," camped in nearby Monitor Valley in 1969, the same year as their ghastly Tate and LaBianca murders in Los Angeles. Ironically, along with his name and date, Manson also carved the peace symbol made famous in the 1960s.

Above: The Combination Highbridge Mill east of Belmont was dismantled in 1914 to erect the second Monitor-Belmont Mill.

Pages 270-271: The second Monitor-Belmont Mill, often mistakenly called the Highbridge Mill, was built in 1915 using Combination Highbridge Mill bricks. Its stark walls are a favorite subject of photographers.

On a hill east of downtown Belmont is a replica, dedicated in 2001, of the 1874 Catholic church that was moved in 1906 to the nearby pioneer town of Manhattan, where it still stands.

Belmont's most photogenic ruins lie east of town. From the town's flagpole, head east, where in .9 of a mile, you'll see the ruins and ninety-foot brick stack of the 1867 Combination Highbridge Mill, a forty-stamp mill that was dismantled in 1914. Beyond those ruins .2 of a mile is a dirt road heading south. In .6 of a mile, you'll come to the dramatic brick skeleton of the second Monitor-Belmont Mill, which was constructed in 1915 using the brick from the Combination Highbridge Mill. This flotation mill, which failed after only two years of operation, is often incorrectly referred to as the Highbridge Mill; it even appears as such on the 1971 Belmont East USGS Topographic Map.

The Belmont Cemetery is kept well trimmed by local volunteers, making it one of Nevada's more attractive ghost town graveyards.

You passed the turnoff to the cemetery as you entered Belmont. Drive .9 of a mile south from Belmont's flagpole and turn east on Cemetery Road. Proceed south along the cemetery's western fence and turn east to the main gate.

The Belmont Cemetery is a well-kept, attractive graveyard, with pines and junipers nicely trimmed by volunteers. Several wooden picket fences surround headstones. As a reminder that some mistakes are indeed "carved in stone," there's an attractive IOOF marker for Andrew Anderson, who died in 1886 at age sixty-five. He was a native of "Sweeden."

BELMONT

WHEN YOU GO

From Tonopah, which is 118 miles south of Austin, drive 5 miles east on U.S. Highway 6 to the junction of Nevada Highway 376. Proceed north for 12.8 miles, where Nevada Secondary Route 882, the clearly marked road to Belmont, heads northeast. Belmont is 26.3 miles from that turnoff. The road is paved all the way to Belmont, but not beyond.

GOLDFIELD

Two turn-of-the-twentieth-century towns, Goldfield and Tonopah, came to the rescue of Nevada. The boom-and-bust cycle of gold and silver mining had caused a severe depression in Nevada in the 1880s that lasted for almost twenty years and emptied the state of a third of its population. That bleak period ended when enormous gold strikes were found in 1900 in Tonopah. Two years later, a Shoshone Indian propector named Tom Fisherman showed Tonopah prospectors Billy Marsh and Harry Stimler gold-laden samples from hills more than thirty miles south of the booming town.

In blowing alkali dust, Marsh and Stimler went to Fisherman's find and discovered gold on what would become known as Columbia Mountain. In honor of the weather, they called their initial claim the Sandstorm. They felt sure they had a true bonanza and made camp, calling the place Grandpa, because they felt this would be what all prospectors seek: "the granddaddy of all gold fields."

Prospectors flocked to the area the following fall. By the end of 1903, Grandpa had been renamed Goldfield because early citizens felt the latter name would be much easier to promote to attract new investors. They were correct; the stampede was on, because the rumors were true and the deposits were deep. By August 1904, mines were producing a stunning ten thousand dollars per day in gold.

With such a promising future, Goldfield rapidly became a city of permanence. Stone and brick edifices were erected. Residences had electricity and

The Goldfield Hotel is an appropriate symbol of the boom-and-bust nature of mining towns: The massive 1908 brick structure at one time served lobster to wealthy patrons. Later it became a near-flophouse as Goldfield dried up. It is vacant at this writing.

running water. The Tonopah & Goldfield Railroad was completed in 1905, assuring a reliable way to get the gold to market. On the return trip, it brought necessities—and luxuries—to a city that was approaching twenty thousand citizens. Eventually, Goldfield was served by four railroads.

By 1907, Goldfield was the largest city in Nevada, with four schools, many four- and five-story buildings, and two exchanges where mining stocks were madly bought and sold with every new rumor.

The Goldfield Hotel, completed in 1908, was the final jewel that exemplified the town's exalted status. It cost almost a half million dollars to build—a four-story brick beauty that featured 154 rooms, a lobby adorned in mahogany, and a dining room where patrons feasted on oysters and lobster.

And the gold just kept on coming. The output in 1909 was nine million dollars, double that of the previous year, and in 1910, the mines produced almost eleven million dollars in gold, bettering the impressive showing of the previous year.

The very nature of mining towns, however, is that they are created only eventually to fail. In 1913, a flood from a desert monsoon damaged many structures in Goldfield, which were never rebuilt. Gold deposits faltered, and production never again approached the peak year of 1910. In 1918, when the one-hundred-stamp Consolidated Mill stopped production, Goldfield began to fade. A huge fire in 1923 destroyed fifty-three square blocks of the town, but Goldfield was moribund long before that. But what a glorious run it had been: In fifteen years of production, the Goldfield Mining District had yielded more than eighty million dollars of the precious metal and was, for that period, the most important gold-producing district in the state. And Goldfield mining was not completely dead—a more modest output of about four hundred thousand dollars per year lasted from 1927 until 1940.

WALKING AND DRIVING AROUND GOLDFIELD

If you are coming from Tonopah, you will notice, before you enter Goldfield, the huge step-up-the-hill foundations of the Goldfield Consolidated Mines Company mill on the side of Columbia Mountain.

As the highway takes a bend to the east entering downtown Goldfield, you can see, on your right, the 1908 West Crook Avenue School, which now serves as the town's library.

The highway into town becomes Crook Avenue, and at the northeast corner of Crook and Columbia Street is the town's landmark building: the Goldfield Hotel. It operated into the 1940s, going from the most elegant hotel found between

The Nixon and Wingfield Block, with its graceful diagonal northwest corner, was constructed in 1907 by two powerful Goldfield entrepreneurs, Senator George Nixon and George Wingfield.

Goldfield High School, built in 1907, badly needs preserving and restoring, but the costs to the private owners are daunting.

Chicago and San Francisco in Goldfield's heyday to almost a flophouse during the lean times. Several people with grandiose plans have sunk thousands upon thousands of dollars into the hotel, but at this writing it is closed to the public.

Two blocks east of the hotel, on the northeast corner of Crook and Euclid avenues, stands the Esmeralda County Courthouse. The stone block fortress-like building opened in 1908, and its main attraction is the second floor's district courtroom, which is elegantly appointed with dark wood and gold trim. Despite its decline in population, Goldfield has remained the county seat almost by default, because no other town in the county rivals even its reduced size. (Esmeralda County is one of the least-populated counties in the contiguous United States.)

The Firehouse Museum, on the southeast corner of Crook and Euclid, features a fire truck, an ambulance, antique fire equipment, and other memorabilia in the former Goldfield Fire Station No. 1.

East of the firehouse, on the southwest corner of Crook and Franklin avenues, is the elaborate, 1906 brick home of George Lewis "Tex" Rickard, owner of the Northern Saloon. Rickard became a promoter of Goldfield in general, but, more famously, a promoter of boxing on the national scene. In 1906, he and other entrepreneurs raised thirty thousand dollars to bring to Goldfield the light-heavyweight championship of the world, which featured defending champion Joe Gans, an African-American from Baltimore, against Danish-born challenger

Oscar "Battling" Nelson. Gans won in an epic bout, a forty-two-rounder decided when Nelson threw an illegal low blow. The resulting nationwide publicity brought newfound respect for the cosmopolitan nature of Goldfield.

From Rickard's house, head south on Franklin one block and drive west for two blocks on Myers Avenue. On the southeast corner of Myers and Fifth avenues stands the attractive 1908 cut-stone home of Charles Kline, a local masonry contractor. The house was sold in 1913 to Frank L. Beard, who had come to Goldfield in 1907 and remained there until his death in 1945.

From the Kline/Beard house, head one block west to Columbia and go north past the Goldfield Hotel. Cross Crook Avenue and proceed one block north to view three excellent buildings. On the southeast corner of Columbia and Ramsey avenues is the handsome, three-story, cut-stone Nixon and Wingfield Block, built in 1907. It served as the headquarters of the Goldfield Consolidated Mines Company and features a graceful, curving northwest corner where its entrance stands on the diagonal.

Next door to that structure on Ramsey is the one-story Southern Nevada Consolidated Telephone-Telegraph Company Building, built in 1906. From here, Goldfield's booms and busts were relayed to the nation's anxious stockholders.

Next door to the Nixon and Wingfield Block on Columbia stands the 1907 three-story Registration Trust Company Building, which also housed the John S. Cook Bank. The building, at this writing, is privately owned and occupied but is open to the public on occasion.

East of those three buildings, on the northwest corner of Ramsey and Euclid avenues, is the photogenic Goldfield High School, erected in 1907. During Goldfield's short bonanza years, it served four hundred students annually. It was condemned in the 1940s. Esmeralda County currently has no high school. Students are bused to Tonopah, the seat of Nye County.

The cemetery is west of town. Take U.S. Highway 95 toward Tonopah, where a sign will direct you to the graveyard, which will be visible to the west, not long after the highway turns from west to north.

The Goldfield Cemetery is made up of many sections, including the Sacred Heart (Catholic), the Knights of Pythias, Elks Rest, Odd Fellows, and the Masons. To the southwest of the main cemetery is a section for the Goldfield Pioneers. These were graves disinterred and moved from downtown to this location in 1908, when the Las Vegas & Tonopah Railroad needed the land for its depot. A sign at the Pioneer Cemetery mentions that those who had the grim job of relocating the graves were known as "official ghouls."

One grave in the main section of the newer cemetery is well worth visiting. As you enter the graveyard, count five rows to the west. On the right will be a large Joshua tree. Next to it is a marker with a child's wagon, reading

Daughter
Mildred Joy Fleming
Born 1897 in Colorado
Died 30 August 1907 Goldfield Nevada

The stone was placed in the 1960s, but an earlier stone is behind it. The grave is for the daughter of Anne Ellis, author of one of the best accounts ever written of the pioneer Western experience, *The Life of an Ordinary Woman*. She spent most of her years in Colorado, much of that time in Bonanza. (Consult my book *Ghost Towns of Colorado* for more on that part of her life). Ellis spent a short time in Goldfield, and while there, her young daughter Joy was stricken with diphtheria and died. In the most moving account in her book, Ellis describes borrowing a child's wagon and hauling a stepping stone she had stolen from the Sundog School's construction site to her home. Ellis had no stonemason's tools but only a large nail to engrave the word "JOY." She then paid an expressman seventy-five cents to help her deliver the stone to the cemetery.

A kitchen sink in a Goldfield miner's cabin has dusty utilitarian dishes ready for a washing that never came.

The dining area of the same cabin shows the mean circumstances in which many Goldfield miners lived.

WHEN YOU GO

Goldfield is 36 miles south of Tonopah on U.S. Highway 95.

GOLD POINT

The town now known as Gold Point had its name changed several times depending upon what was being mined there. Originally, when lime deposits were found in 1868, the small community that grew near the deposits was called Lime Point. Silver was discovered in the 1880s, but the silver was thoroughly embedded in surrounding rock, making it unprofitable to mine. Discoveries in Tonopah and Goldfield at the turn of the twentieth century, however, brought renewed interest in the surrounding hills.

As a result of this more intense examination, significant amounts of silver were found at Lime Point in 1905, followed by a bonanza of high-grade horn silver in 1908. As miners descended upon the site, the camp became known as Hornsilver. Eventually, it became a town featuring more than two hundred wood-frame buildings with the usual stores, thirteen saloons, and a post office. The town's growth was hampered somewhat by never having a railroad; the nearest station was at Ralston, fifteen miles east.

Gold was discovered in 1927 within the Great Western silver mine, and by the 1930s, when more gold was being mined than silver, Hornsilver became Gold Point. But when World War II began, the federal government closed mines of non-strategic metals. Gold Point became a ghost, but not before more than a million dollars in gold and silver had been extricated from its mines.

WALKING AROUND GOLD POINT

As mentioned in this chapter's introduction, Gold Point is this book's finest example of an early mining camp that is not part of a state park. Most camps like it have long since disappeared. But Gold Point contains more than three dozen buildings, most of them tiny miners' quarters, along with some rudimentary commercial structures. For this preservation, we can thank many former residents and volunteers, but special gratitude goes to two people: Ora Mae Wiley, who moved to Gold Point in 1930 and watched over the town until her death, at age eighty-three, in 1980; and Herb Robbins, who started buying Gold Point buildings in 1980 and is still there at this writing, carefully shoring up and restoring his properties.

On the west side of town are photogenic false-front, wood-frame buildings, including Mitchell's Mercantile, the Expiration Mercantile, and the Turf Saloon and

Gold Point's false-front buildings are the kind that, if not protected, will disappear into the desert. These have survived in part because of the present owner, Coleen Garland.

Grill, all dating from about 1908. A block south of those buildings is the picturesque 1908 Gold Dust Saloon and a series of miners' residences. One block east is the post office—which closed in 1967—along with some carefully restored miners' cabins (occasionally available for lodging) and the attractive Hornsilver Townsite and Telephone Building, now a saloon. Many mining artifacts and an eclectic array of fire engines placed throughout the town add to the charm of Gold Point.

WHEN YOU GO

From Goldfield, head south on U.S. Highway 95 for 13.5 miles to Lida Junction. Turn southwest on Nevada Highway 266 and drive 7 miles to Nevada Highway 774, the road to Gold Point, which is just beyond a state historical marker. Gold Point is 7.2 miles southwest of that marker.

RHYOLITE

Frank "Shorty" Harris (1856 to 1934) was one of Death Valley's most colorful characters. He was a charmer, a braggart, a drunk, and a man with a knack for finding mineral wealth in one of the Earth's most desolate places. He also, unfortunately, had a knack for boasting endlessly about his strikes, ensuring that the riches ended up in the hands of others who rushed to his discoveries while Shorty drank to his newfound wealth. His memory is etched in Death Valley at Harrisburg, named for him; at Ballarat, where he was the sole resident before his death; and at a spot just north of the Eagle Borax Works, where Shorty is buried, at his request, next to his friend Jimmy Dayton, who had been buried there for more than thirty years before Harris' death.

Shorty's most dramatic discovery was made in 1904, when he and fellow prospector Ernest "Ed" Cross found gold at what they would call the Bullfrog claim because the first piece of rock had a greenish tint and was about the size of a bullfrog. Shorty crowed to his buddies that the find was a "crackerjack" and added, "The district is going to be the banner camp of Nevada!" The two went to have their ore assayed in Goldfield. Harris, in a drunken celebration of their find, apparently sold his half for a mere $1,000, which he immediately squandered. Cross held on and did much better, eventually selling his claim for a reported $125,000. He used the money to buy a large ranch in Escondido, near San Diego. Harris was out of the picture and continued prospecting in Death Valley for his next big strike, which never came.

The real jackpot was located a couple of miles north of the Bullfrog claim, and the strike at the Montgomery Shoshone Mine made E. A. "Bob" Montgomery Death Valley's first mining millionaire. The town that formed nearby was called Rhyolite in honor of the silica-laden volcanic rock found in the area.

By 1908, the Bullfrog Mining District was a true bonanza. In addition to Rhyolite were the satellite communities of Bullfrog, Gold Center, and Beatty. Population estimates of Rhyolite vary widely, from four thousand to double that number. The town could boast of all the modern conveniences, including electricity, telephones, and abundant running water, which was piped from springs at the source of the Amargosa River, one of the world's longest underground rivers. Rhyolite featured a stock exchange, a board of trade, the Miners' Union

This mercantile at Rhyolite was built in 1906 of rudimentary materials. It is east of Golden Street, where the town's more elaborate places of business stood.

Hospital, an ice plant, stores and hotels, the First Presbyterian and St. Mary's Catholic churches, the Arcade Opera House, the highly popular Alaska Glacier Ice Cream Parlor, and three public swimming pools.

Three railroads eventually served Rhyolite: the Las Vegas & Tonopah, the Tonopah & Tidewater, and the Bullfrog & Goldfield.

Even as all these refinements were blossoming in Rhyolite, most of the mines in the Bullfrog District were quickly tapping out. The big exception was the Montgomery Shoshone, which was the mainstay of Rhyolite, producing more than one million dollars in bullion in just three years. Virtually none of the stockholders, however, received a penny in dividends because of stock speculation and questionable financial dealings. Stock in the Montgomery Shoshone went from twenty-three dollars per share to a mere three dollars even as the mine was making money. By 1911, with the ore playing out, the stock value plummeted to four cents per share.

The financial demise of the Montgomery Shoshone and its subsequent closing was the final blow for the once-booming Bullfrog District. The last train left

Rhyolite in 1913, the same year the post office closed. The Nevada-California Power Company took down its power lines in 1916.

WALKING AND DRIVING AROUND RHYOLITE

As you drive up the wide dirt road from Nevada Highway 374, you will pass a turnoff .7 of a mile from the highway. That will take you to the town-site of Bullfrog, where there is one modern building and one ruin. It is also the route to the Bullfrog-Rhyolite Cemetery. More on that later.

The remnants of Rhyolite begin .7 of a mile north of the turnoff to Bullfrog. The site is managed by the Bureau of Land Management, and occasionally volunteer caretakers oversee the site. If volunteers are there, they will likely be near the 1906 Tom T. Kelly Bottle House, which was erected in less than six months principally using Adolphus Busch beer bottles—about thirty thousand of them. A walking tour handout may be available at the restored bottle house, which is surrounded by elaborate fencing worthy of a high-security prison. Next door is a former general store.

The main drag through town is Golden Street, where Rhyolite's most dramatic ruins reside, including the roofless, concrete, two-story schoolhouse, built in 1909 and the last major building to be erected in Rhyolite. When it was finished, the town was already beginning to empty, and the school was never at capacity.

North of the schoolhouse are the foundations and walls of once-three-story Overbury Block. Across the street is the lonely façade of the 1906 Porter Brothers Store. H. D. and L. D. Porter brought

The John S. Cook Bank remains one of Nevada's most photographed ruins. It has appeared in everything from music videos to Hollywood movies.

The Las Vegas & Tonopah Railroad Depot awaits extensive renovation. The Bureau of Land Management hopes that the landmark building will eventually be the centerpiece of Rhyolite.

merchandise across Death Valley from their store in Randsburg, California, and purchased a lot in Rhyolite for the then-outrageous sum of twelve hundred dollars. Their store became the favorite of Rhyolite's citizens, a place where, according to the Porter brothers, "We handle all good things except whiskey."

Up the street stands the 1908 John S. Cook Bank, one of the most photographed ghost town structures in the American West. (This is the same John S. Cook who also had a bank, still standing, in Goldfield [see page 279].) The jagged ruins have appeared in calendars, television shows, and movies. In its prime, the three-story building featured Italian marble floors, Honduran mahogany woodwork, and stained glass windows. The bank occupied the first floor, brokerage offices filled the upper floors, and the Rhyolite post office was in the basement.

Farther up Golden Street is the most imposing—and, at $130,000, the most expensive—edifice in town, the 1909 Las Vegas & Tonopah Railroad Depot. At this writing, it is unceremoniously surrounded by a chain-link fence, but there are hopes of eventually restoring it and opening it to the public.

If you follow a dirt road southeast from the depot, you will come around to two substantial buildings, a 1907 rock residence that perhaps was a brothel and, nearby, the 1907 concrete jail. As you walk or drive the back streets of town, you'll see many signs pointing out what once stood at various locations.

As mentioned earlier, you passed the turnoff to the cemetery on your way into town. Return to that junction, turn west, and head .3 of a mile to the old railroad grade heading south. Down that grade .6 of a mile is the turnoff east to the Bullfrog-Rhyolite Cemetery, where you will find about two dozen graves marked by either a fence, a headstone, or both. The most unusual marker is a carefully carved cylindrical stone for James C. Clayton (1866 to 1905), who died just as Rhyolite began to boom.

H. D. and L. D. Porter erected a general store in then-booming Rhyolite in 1906. Theirs was the most popular store of its type in town.

RHYOLITE

WHEN YOU GO

Rhyolite is 3.9 miles southwest of Beatty on Nevada Highway 374. Beatty is 68 miles southeast of the Lida Junction turnoff to Gold Point, 83 miles southeast of Goldfield, and 116 miles northwest of Las Vegas.

Note: *The ghost towns of Death Valley are nearby, southwest of Rhyolite. You can track them down with one of my earlier books,* Southern California's Best Ghost Towns.

BERLIN

Berlin was a late addition to a series of mining camps that sprouted in the Union Mining District beginning in 1863. The original towns included Union, Ione, and Grantsville. Although Berlin Canyon was prospected in 1869, mining did not begin there until 1895 when silver was extracted from the Berlin Mine.

A consolidation of area mines by the Nevada Company in 1908 brought Berlin to prominence, with a population of between two hundred and three hundred people. A thirty-stamp mill was the town's largest building, but the community also featured a post office, a stage station, an assay office, a union hall, and miners' residences. The historical photos I have seen show only wood-frame buildings, but Fermin Bruner, who lived in the camp as a child, reported that Louie Chirac lived in a two-story brick building, the second story of which was occasionally used for community dances.

Berlin was virtually dead by 1909, although a cyanide plant was built to work the mill's tailings for three years beginning in 1911.

WALKING AND DRIVING AROUND BERLIN

Berlin is a part of the Berlin Ichthyosaur State Park and is listed on the National Register of Historic Places. A modest fee is required to enter, payable at the park headquarters, which is located in the former mine supervisor's office. You will be given a brochure of a walking tour of the townsite, which includes, among twelve standing buildings, the assay office, the stage station, a machine shop, and the huge shell of the Berlin Mill. The mill was stripped of its equipment during World War II as part of a national salvage effort. And Louie Chirac's large brick building? When a mining town is abandoned, brick is one of the first commodities to be salvaged and used elsewhere.

A path leads to the town's cemetery southeast of town.

Fossils of ichthyosaurs, fifty-foot-long prehistoric marine reptiles, were discovered near Berlin in 1928 and excavated from 1954 into the 1960s. They are the largest ichthyosaur specimens ever found.

Berlin, now inside a Nevada state park, includes, among many others, these three buildings, left to right: the assay office, the machine shop, and the Berlin Mill.

WHEN YOU GO

Gabbs is 111 miles northwest of Tonopah via U.S. Highway 6, U.S. Highway 95, and Nevada Highway 361. From Gabbs, drive north on Highway 361 for 2.8 miles and turn right onto Nevada Highway 844. Follow that road for 16 miles to a clearly marked turnoff to Berlin. The townsite, which will have been visible for many miles across the Ione Valley high on the side of the Shoshone Mountains, is 2.1 miles from the turnoff.

VIRGINIA CITY

Virginia City is the living, historic reminder of one of the greatest silver finds in the history of the world. Its famous Comstock Lode helped finance the Union in the Civil War; it provided backing for the Transcontinental Railroad and the Atlantic telegraph cables; and it helped make San Francisco a jewel of the West.

Brothers Hosea and Ethan Allen Grosch may have been the first to find gold, and then a promising vein of silver quartz, in the sagebrush-filled hills of what was then called the Washoe in 1852. Their letter home to family in Pennsylvania expressed optimism about their find, with an assay of three thousand dollars of silver to the ton. In 1857, however, Hosea accidentally pierced his foot with his pick while working their claim. His foot subsequently became infected, and he was dead within two weeks. His grief-stricken brother abandoned the claim and headed off to California over the Sierra Nevada. Like many in the Donner Party eleven years before, he was caught by winter weather and froze to death.

By the mid-1850s, a few prospectors were working the same area as the Grosches' discovery. They were hampered by a kind of sludge that was referred to as "blasted blue stuff," a metallic conglomeration that covered the mercury that normally helped separate gold in the bottom of their rockers. The primitive camp that formed around their diggings was known as Johntown, a hodgepodge of shacks and tents that saw more and more hopeful newcomers attempting to find placer gold in the nearby canyons.

Stories vary about who found the first real bonanza and how they did it. One popular version begins in January 1859 when Virginia native James "Old Virginny" Finney (or Fenemore) and Henry T. Paige "Old Pancake" Comstock located placer claims without knowing that rich primary deposits lay beneath the surface. Eventually those deposits gave a name to the entire area: The Comstock Lode.

Another version leaves Old Virginny out of the picture and has Peter O'Riley and Patrick McLaughlin finding gold in the spring of 1859, along with "heavy black stuff" (the same "blasted blue stuff" hated by prospectors a few years earlier). In this version, however, Henry Comstock came along and said they were on his land. Fearing to be cut out entirely, they offered to cut him in. Comstock agreed for a good reason: His claim was a bluff. He had title to nothing.

Virginia City's citizens wanted to impress visitors with buildings that exuded splendor, permanence, and wealth. The 1876 Storey County Courthouse is a prime example.

C Street is the main thoroughfare in Virginia City. Most of these elaborate buildings, with their ironwork façades and fancy cornices, date from the mid-1870s.

A few months later, two visitors to the Comstock claim asked about the "black stuff." Comstock told them it was worse than worthless, because it hampered the process of gold recovery. The two men, out of curiosity, took a sample of the sludge-like clay to an assay office in Grass Valley, California. The clay was laden with sulphurites of silver. It was worth three thousand dollars per ton in silver and another eight hundred dollars per ton in gold. The Comstock Lode had gold, all right, but it also contained the richest silver deposit America had ever seen. When word got out, California miners working the nearly tapped-out gold fields of the 1849 strikes were on the move to the Washoe along with farmers, merchants, and—to lead them all to their jackpot—thousands of prospectors.

In 1850, the territory that would become Nevada had a population of—apart from the nomadic Native Americans who occasionally camped there—about a dozen people. After the silver discoveries of the Comstock Lode, the population rose to 6,857 in 1860, to 42,491 in 1870, and to about 75,000 by 1875. Several camps sprouted in addition to the shanties of Johntown, including Gold Hill, Silver City, and Como. One of the smaller camps, likely named for that early prospector Old Virginny, was destined to eclipse them all: Virginia City.

The four men mentioned as the possible discoverers of the great lode did not fare well with the bonanza. Old Virginny Finney lived for only two years after probably providing the name for his town. He was killed when he fell off a horse in a drunken stupor. Henry Comstock, who provided the name for the famous lode, sold his share of the claim for $11,000. He squandered it and eventually committed suicide with a pistol. Patrick McLaughlin sold out for a mere $3,500. When he died, he was a cook on a ranch in Montana. Peter O'Riley held out for $40,000, but he fared no better. At the end of his life, he was an inmate of an insane asylum.

Chronicler of the West J. Ross Browne visited fledgling Virginia City in 1860 and described it as made up of "frame shanties, pitched together as if by accident; tents of canvas, of blankets, of brush, of potato sacks and old shirts with empty whisky-barrels for chimneys, smoky hovels of wood and stone; coyote holes in the mountain side forcibly seized and held by men; pits and shafts with smoke issuing from every crevice."

Virginia City, however, was not to remain a crude camp for long. Roads were built to haul goods in and silver ore out. Financiers and mining professionals

Mine superintendent Robert Graves created this showplace residence, now known simply as "The Castle," in 1868.

The Silver Terrace Cemeteries of Virginia City used to be a verdant parklike place. Virginia City itself is in the background.

brought expertise to tap the vast lode. A German engineer, Philip Diedesheimer, invented a timbering process known as the square-set, a clever bracing system that allowed Comstock mines to follow veins in any direction and to seemingly any depth.

Virginia City's apparently endless wealth brought in refinements that smaller camps never had—opulent mansions for mine owners, a beautiful courthouse, an extravagant opera house, a costly schoolhouse, three lovely churches, and elegant restaurants and saloons. Of course, the burgeoning city also had slums, a red-light district, and a criminal element, along with noise and pollution. But those were merely necessary evils outshone by the sunlight of prodigious prosperity.

One of America's most beloved literary figures began his writing career in Virginia City. Samuel Clemens took a job writing for the *Territorial Enterprise* in 1862, a position he held for only two years before moving to San Francisco to work for four newspapers. While in Virginia City, he first used the *nom de plume* Mark Twain. By 1869, after only seven years as a writer, he was a national sensation for his travel narrative *Innocents Abroad*.

But back to Virginia City. Just when the bonanza seemed about to fade, new discoveries brought Virginia City back to life. In 1869, new silver strikes brought the Virginia & Truckee Railroad from Carson City. That same year saw the first work on the Sutro Tunnel, built by Adolph Sutro to ventilate the mines and drain them of water. In 1871, a new rich vein was found in the Crown Point Mine. Two years later, the biggest strike of all was made in the Consolidated Virginia Mine— a bonanza that yielded more than one hundred million dollars in silver. It made millionaires of miners John Mackay and James Fair along with their eventual partners—two members of the San Francisco Stock Exchange, James Flood and William O'Brien.

These enormous silver strikes sent Virginia City to even greater glory. Now a city of about twenty thousand citizens (almost a tenth of them Chinese), it could boast of six churches, five newspapers, four banks, fifty mercantiles—and more than a hundred saloons.

Opposite: Solomon Noel, who died in 1896 at age fifty-eight, is memorialized with the touching figure of a woman who holds a bouquet in her left arm as she drops a rose with her right.

SOLOMON NOEL
DIED
SEPT 22, 1896,
AGED
56 YEARS.

The Great Fire, in October 1875, took out two-thirds of the buildings in town. Although much of Virginia City was rebuilt, it never approached its former glory. In the peak year of 1876, Virginia City mines produced $38 million in ore. The four-mile-long Sutro Tunnel was completed in 1879, but the peak was already over. By 1881, silver production had fallen to only $1.4 million. By 1899, the total was a mere $172,000.

Between 1859 and 1878—only nineteen spectacular years—Virginia City mines produced well over $300 million in silver and gold. After that period, mines worked sporadically for another sixty-two years, yielding another estimated $100 million in riches.

WALKING AND DRIVING AROUND VIRGINIA CITY

The main thoroughfare in Virginia City is C Street, which features shops, former hotels, saloons, casinos, restaurants, and museums—all hoping to see your credit card. Many of Virginia City's attractions require an admission fee. For my reaction to their merits versus their expense, see pages 304 to 306. But the buildings themselves are the real stars of downtown, so be sure to look at the elaborate cornices, the interesting window treatments, and the elaborate metal façades. On the bottom corners of several façades are dates and places of manufacture. Virtually all of these buildings were erected in 1875 or 1876 to outdo the competition.

One block west of C Street is B Street, which features the 1876 Storey County Courthouse, the oldest continuously operating courthouse in Nevada. Next door is the 1885 Piper's Opera House, where luminaries such as Buffalo Bill Cody, Lily Langtry, Edwin Booth, and Sarah Bernhardt performed. This opera house is the third to stand in this location; the other two burned in 1875 and 1883, respectively.

A few blocks south on C Street stands the 1868 mansion owned by Robert Graves, a mine superintendent. Now known simply as The Castle, it has an elegant carriage house that mimics the architecture of the mansion itself. It is private and closed to the public at this writing, as are all the major mansions in town. I certainly hope that changes; I toured the lovely John Mackay Mansion (at D and Washington streets) in 1980 and thoroughly enjoyed it.

Virginia City has three historic churches. The late-1860s Presbyterian church, located south of the main business district on C Street, was the only one to escape the Great Fire of 1875. St. Paul's Episcopal Church, on F Street at Taylor, was erected in 1876 to replace one that was lost in that same conflagration. Across the intersection from the Episcopal church is St. Mary's in the Mountains Catholic Church, an enormous, elaborate monument from Virginia City's generous parishioners, prominently including millionaire John Mackay, who underwrote the rebuilding of the church after the 1875 fire.

Virginia City's 1867 Silver Terrace Cemeteries stand northeast of town off of Carson Street. A brochure, which should be available at the main entrance, tells you that in Virginia City's heyday, the graveyard featured flower gardens, flowing water, and paths for respectful contemplation. It was, in effect, the community's city park. Eleven separate cemeteries are located within the Silver Terrace, including sections for the Odd Fellows, the Knights of Pythias, the Masons, and for those buried by the Wilson and Brown Funeral House.

One unusual graveyard in the Silver Terrace is the Exempt Fireman's Cemetery. A sign at the entrance explains that a fireman could retire, or go "exempt," after twenty years of service. He didn't have to respond to calls, but he enjoyed all the other benefits and privileges of active service, including the right to be buried in this place of honor.

WHEN YOU GO

From Reno, take U.S. Highway 395 south for about nine miles to Nevada Highway 341. Take Highway 341 for 14 miles to Virginia City. From Carson City, drive west on U.S. Highway 50 for about 8 miles and turn north on Highway 341. Virginia City is 8 miles north.

Note: The best ghost town in the West (but outside of the Mountain West parameters of this book), California's Bodie, is less than 125 miles from Virginia City. For more information on Bodie and the towns of the '49er Gold Rush, consult my book Ghost Towns of Northern California.

Virginia City Attractions

You can spend a lot of money in Virginia City, and dozens of businesses are there to help you do just that. I decided to become the ultimate tourist in a tourism machine and visit virtually every attraction in town. The easiest way to do that is to go to the Virginia City Convention and Tourism Authority building at the northwest corner of Taylor and C streets and purchase its deluxe ticket booklet. The pleasant ladies in that office suggested that I use the tram tour ticket first, since I would get an overall picture of the town and see many of the attractions I would later visit. That was excellent advice.

What follows is my assessment of the attractions in the ticket packet, ranked in order of what I considered the most entertainment value for the money. (Since maps of the town are available in the tourism authority and other places, I am not giving directions.) Naturally, if you buy the booklet, the attractions then seem free, so to speak, but you do feel obligated to experience them all since you have paid for them. To visit all the attractions in one day would be exhausting. Unless you are going to stay overnight (I stayed three nights and loved the experience), I wouldn't buy the deluxe booklet. Where, then, should you spend your money if you don't have enough time to visit them all? Here are my recommendations:

1. **The Virginia & Truckee Railroad:** I love tourist train rides, so perhaps I'm not a fair judge, but this attraction offered the best value for my tourist dollar. Our trip was powered by a 1916 Baldwin steam locomotive, a big plus over a diesel operation, and the train went through a tunnel, which is always enjoyable. The ride, at this writing, takes only thirty-five minutes, which might be an advantage for parents with children. I watched the delight on two young faces as they took their first train ride, which was short enough that they were engaged throughout. Eventually, however, the train will go all the way to Carson City, a route the railroad last traversed in 1938. In our short version, the train backed down to neighboring Gold Hill, so the soot and smoke trailed harmlessly behind. But on the uphill return trip, we had the thrill (and the smell, the smoke, and the

soot—even within the covered car) of the power of a steam locomotive. It was exhilarating.

2. **The Comstock Mill:** I have rated this attraction so highly because it is, at this writing, unique in America. It is the only stamp mill tour that actually operates, and for me, that was a delight. Other tours show mills only in repose, but this one fires up, with long flapping belts connecting various elements, two stamps pounding away at the ore coming through, and a shaker table madly vibrating to separate the precious metal from the detritus. Whether you think you are interested in mills or not, I would give this a try. You will be amazed at the ingenuity involved in this nineteenth-century contraption.

3. **The Fourth Ward School Museum:** The star attraction of this museum is the building itself, a three-story Victorian gem that served students from 1876 until 1936. The third story, at this writing, is closed to the public, but the first and second stories feature, among other exhibits, a well-preserved original classroom, with central pot-bellied stove; displays on the history of the Comstock Lode; a showcase of women's clothing; and a section on the role of minorities in Virginia City.

4. **Virginia City Trolley or Tram Tour:** As mentioned earlier, this is the first attraction I visited, and I suggest you do the same. Our driver-narrator was informative and entertaining. On the twenty-minute tour, you pass most of the places mentioned here—and many others—and learn a great deal about the history of Virginia City.

5. **The Nevada Gambling Museum:** Nevada is best-known for its gaming meccas, so here's a chance to learn something about gambling. This attraction is very inexpensive, costing less than a one-minute foray with a slot machine (of which you will see hundreds after you step inside). My favorite section was on cheating devices, especially the Sleeve Hold Out, something you definitely would not want to be caught wearing in a card game.

6. **The Way It Was Museum:** The amount of memorabilia in this museum is simply overwhelming—and that's not necessarily good. I spent about thirty minutes inside, but I could have consumed hours and still not seen it all. If you're willing to spend the time, it's a fascinating place. But I kept thinking about all the other attractions I had paid for and felt a bit frustrated. The blacksmith

shop is well worth examining, and I enjoyed reading the labels in the pharmaceuticals section to see what amazing promises were made for some products that were clearly "snake oil."

7. **The Ponderosa Mine Tour:** This book mentions seven mine tours, and the Ponderosa falls somewhere in the middle. The tour is unique in that the entrance is inside a building: the former Bank of California Building, now the Ponderosa Saloon. We were offered a protective miner's helmet, but it wasn't required wearing. We proceeded in about three hundred feet of easy walking, with stops along the way to view various displays. Our guide was very informative but was hard to hear in the tunnel.

8. **The Mark Twain Museum:** It was a thrill for this writer and former English teacher to descend the very steps that Mark Twain once took. But unless you are interested in old printing press equipment, this attraction has limited appeal.

9. **The Radio Museum:** If you are fascinated with old radio and Citizens' Band equipment, this is for you. Unfortunately, I don't share that fascination.

10. **The Chollar Mine Tour:** This mine tour was inferior to the Ponderosa. We were not offered protective headgear, and we could have used it because the mine timbers are rather low. The passageway is quite uneven and is wet and slick in spots. You're also competing for space with a large air duct. This is no place for anyone uncertain of foot. You walk in a stooped position for four hundred feet into the mine and then stand in one spot, get good information about the mining process, and then walk back out.

The Comstock Fire Museum: This deserves a special mention, since it would be up at number three or four on this list, except that it's not on the ticket—because it's free (donations accepted). Located in the 1864 Liberty Engine Company No.1 Firehouse, it features several horse-drawn fire wagons, including one from the 1840s, the oldest firefighting apparatus in Nevada. Be sure to examine the incredible brass fittings, the intricate paint striping, and the attention to fine detail on these magnificent machines.

The Fourth Ward School Museum.

ACKNOWLEDGMENTS

For assistance in historical research: Clear Creek Canyon Historical Society of Chaffee County; Colorado Historical Society Library and Barbara Dey and Rebecca Lintz; Denver Public Library Western History Department; Durango & Silverton Narrow Gauge Railroad and Kristi Nelson; Gilpin County Historical Society and James J. Prochaska, Executive Director; Tom Hill, Georgetown Loop Railroad; Marble Historical Society and Joseph Manz, President; San Juan County Historical Society and Beverly Rich, Chairman; Keith Siddel, the Old Firehouse Bed and Breakfast Inn, Creede; Bob Seago and Jan Jacobs, Creede Historical Society; Dan Smith, Park Manager, Land of the Yankee Fork Historic Area, Idaho Department of Parks and Recreation; Roger and Jerri Nelson, the Idaho Hotel, Silver City; Christine Allred, Secretary, Friends of Historic Spring City; Elizabeth Rassiga, Austin; and Jim Price and Angela Haag, Goldfield.

For fieldwork support: Jim Janoviak and Karen Daly, Denver; Sharon Rossino, Executive Director, Hamill House Museum; Carol Davis, Curator, South Park City; Tommy Fraser, Marble and Crystal; Jim and Nancy Thorsen, Idaho Falls; Dan Smith, Park Manager, Land of the Yankee Fork Historic Area, Idaho Department of Parks and Recreation, and employees Jan Haugh and Michelle Fox; Elizabeth Rassiga and Joy Brandt, Austin; Bertie and Henry Berg, and Paula Kniefel, Belmont; Jim Price and Joan Sieber, and Angela Haag, Goldfield; and Herb Robbins and Coleen Garland, Gold Point.

For photographic assistance: Jim Janoviak, Denver; John Walden, Photographics Works Lab, Tucson; and especially to John and Susan Drew, of Wilson, Wyoming—my book partners since 1997. John and Susan took the photographs for my last three books, and their professional expertise and remarkable vision made those books the delight to the eye that they are. They then, in retirement, lent me John's Pentax 6X7 and gave me—*gave* me—almost two hundred rolls of film for this solo project. I did all the photography for my first four books, but working with John and Susan has sharpened my eye and improved my technique. I hope they are satisfied with the results in this book, for they have set the standard very high.

And with grateful thanks to trip companions who have traveled the backroads with me in these six states over the years: Jim Janoviak and Karen Daly, Warren Weaver, MaryAnn Mead, Jim Price and Joan Sieber, and Betty-Ann Craven; and with special thanks to the dozens of friends who found and explored ghost towns with me on mountain bikes.

GLOSSARY OF MINING TERMS

adit: A nearly horizontal entrance to a hard-rock mine.

argonaut: The men who came to California during the Gold Rush (after the Argonauts of Greek mythology who sailed on the ship *Argo* in search of riches).

arrastra: An apparatus used to grind ore by means of a heavy stone that is dragged around in a circle, normally by mules or oxen.

assay: To determine the value of a sample of ore, in ounces per ton, by testing using a chemical evaluation.

bonanza: To miners, a body of rich ore.

charcoal kiln (or oven): A structure into which wood is placed and subjected to intense heat through a controlled, slow burning. Charcoal is a longer-lasting, more efficient fuel than wood and is often used to power mills and smelters. If the kiln is used to convert coal to coke, it's called a "coke oven."

chloride: Usually refers to ores containing chloride of silver.

claim: A tract of land with defined boundaries that includes mineral rights extending downward from the surface.

claim-jumping (or jumping a claim): Illegally taking over someone else's claim.

diggings (or diggins): Evidence of mining efforts, such as placer, hydraulic, or dredge workings.

dredge: An apparatus, usually on a flat-bottomed boat, that scoops material out of a river to extract gold-bearing sand or gravel; used in "dredging" or "dredge mining."

dust: Minute gold particles found in placer deposits.

flotation: A method of mineral separation in a mill in which water, in combination with chemicals, "floats" finely crushed minerals of value to separate them from the detritus, which sinks. Process used in a flotation mill.

flume: An inclined, manmade channel, usually of wood, used to convey water or mine waste, often for long distances.

gallows frame: See "headframe," below.

giant: The nozzle on the end of a pipe through which water is forced in hydraulic mining. Also called a "monitor."

grubstake: An advance of money, food, and/or supplies to a prospector in return for a share of any discoveries.

hard-rock mining: The process in which a primary deposit is mined by removing ore-bearing rock by tunneling into the earth. Also known as quartz mining, since gold is frequently found in quartz deposits.

headframe: The vertical apparatus over a mine shaft that has cables to be lowered down the shaft for raising either ore or a cage; sometimes called a "gallows frame."

high-grade ore: Rich ore.

high-grading: The theft of rich ore, usually by a miner working for someone else who owns the mine.

hopper: In mining, a structure with funnels from which the contents, loaded from above, can be emptied for purposes of transportation.

horn silver: Silver chloride, a native ore of silver. Also known as Cerargyrite.

hydraulic mining: A method of mining using powerful jets of water to wash away a bank of gold-bearing earth. Also known by miners as "hydraulicking."

ingot: A cast bar or block of a metal.

lode: A continuous mineral-bearing deposit or vein (see also "Mother Lode"). In Nevada, the famous lode was the Comstock Lode of Virginia City.

mill: A building in which rock is crushed to extract minerals by one of several methods. If this is done by stamps (heavy hammers or pestles), it is a stamp mill. If by iron balls, it is a ball mill. The mill is usually constructed on the side of a hill to utilize its slope—hence, a "gravity-fed mill."

mining district: An area of land described (usually for legal purposes) and designated as containing valuable minerals in paying amounts.

monitor: See "giant."

Mother Lode: The principal lode passing through a district or section of the country; from the same term in Spanish, *La Veta Madre*. In California, it refers specifically to the hundred-mile-long concentration of gold on the western slopes of the Sierra Nevada.

mucker: A person or machine that clears material such as rock in a mine.

nugget: A lump of native gold or other mineral. The largest found in California's Mother Lode weighed 195 pounds.

ore: A mineral of sufficient concentration, quantity, and value to be mined at a profit.

ore sorter: A structure, usually near a mine, in which higher-grade ore is sorted from lower-grade ore or waste before being sent to the mill or smelter.

pan: To look for placer gold by washing earth, gravel, or sand, usually in a streambed, by using a shallow, concave dish—a "pan."

placer: A waterborne deposit of sand or gravel containing heavier materials such as gold, which have been eroded from their original bedrock and concentrated as small particles that can be washed, or "panned," out (see also "secondary deposit").

pocket: In primary deposits, a small but rich concentration of gold embedded in quartz. In secondary deposits, a hole or indentation in a stream bed in which gold dust or nuggets have been trapped.

powderhouse: A structure placed safely away from a mine that stores such volatile materials as gunpowder or dynamite. The building's walls are usually very stout, but its roof is intentionally of flimsier construction, so if the contents should explode, the main force of the blast would be into the air.

primary deposit: A deposit of gold or other mineral found in its original location. Ore is extracted by hard-rock mining or hydraulic mining.

prospect: Mineral workings of unproven value.

prospector: He who searches for prospects.

quartz mining: See "hard-rock mining."

rocker: A portable sluicebox used by prospectors.

salting: To place valuable minerals in a place in which they do not actually occur. Done to deceive. Therefore, a salted claim is one that is intended to lure the unsuspecting investor into a scam.

secondary deposit: A deposit of gold or other mineral that has moved from its original location by water. Ore is extracted by placer mining or dredging.

shaft: A vertical or nearly vertical opening into the earth for hard-rock mining.

slag: The waste product of a smelter; hence, "slag dumps."

sluicebox: A wooden trough in which placer deposits are sluiced, or "washed," to retrieve gold from the deposits.

smelter: A building or complex in which material is melted in order to separate impurities from pure metal.

square set: A set of timbers that are cut so that they form a ninety-degree angle and so that they can be combined with other "sets" to create a framework that safely buttresses a mine. First used in the Comstock Lode.

strike: The discovery of a primary or secondary deposit of gold or other mineral in sufficient concentration and/or quantity to be mined profitably.

tailings: Waste or refuse left after milling is complete; sometimes used more generally, although incorrectly, to indicate waste dumps. Because of improved technology, older tailings have often been reworked to extract minerals that were left behind from an older, cruder milling process.

tramway: An apparatus for moving materials such as ore, rock, or even supplies in buckets suspended from pulleys that run on a cable.

tunnel: A horizontal or nearly horizontal underground passage open at one end at least.

vein: A zone or belt of valuable mineral within less valuable neighboring rock.

waste dump: Waste rock, not of sufficient value to warrant milling, that comes out of the mine; usually found immediately outside the mine entrance.

workings: A general term indicating any mining development; when that development is exhausted, it is "worked out."

BIBLIOGRAPHY

A Guide to the South Pass Historic Mining Area. South Path City, WY: The Friends of South Pass, Inc., 1978. (Revised by Nancy McClure, 1995.)

Aldrich, John K. *Ghosts of Clear Creek County.* Lakewood, CO: Centennial Graphics, 1984. (Revised 1992.)

————. *Ghosts of Gilpin County.* Lakewood, CO: Centennial Graphics, 1985. (Revised 1996.)

————. *Ghosts of Summit County.* Lakewood, CO: Centennial Graphics, 1986. (Revised 1992.)

————. *Ghosts of the Western San Juans, vol. 1.* Lakewood, CO: Centennial Graphics, 1988. (Revised 1991.)

Arizona Daily Star, January 8, 1995 and May 23, 1999.

Bennett, Earl H. *Geo Note,* no. 37. Moscow, ID: Idaho Geological Survey, n.d.

Bancroft, Caroline. *Augusta Tabor: Her Side of the Scandal.* Boulder, CO: Johnson Books, 1955. (Sixth edition, 1970.)

————. *Unique Ghost Towns and Mountain Spots.* Boulder, CO: Johnson Books, 1961.

Benson, Maxine. *1,001 Colorado Place Names.* Lawrence, KS: University Press of Kansas, 1994.

Bruner, Firmin. *Some Remembered . . . Some Forgot: Life in Central Nevada Mining Camps.* Carson City, NV: Nevada State Park Natural History Association, 1974.

Carr, Stephen L. *The Historical Guide to Utah Ghost Towns.* Salt Lake City: Western Epics, 1972.

Chesher, Greer K. *Historic Grafton* (brochure). Salt Lake City: Utah Division of State History and the National Park Service, n.d.

Dallas, Sandra. *Colorado Ghost Towns and Mining Camps.* Norman, OK: University of Oklahoma Press, 1985.

Denver Post, November 12, 1995.

Desert Magazine, August 1960.

Ellis, Anne. *The Life of an Ordinary Woman.* New York: Houghton Mifflin, 1929. (Reprinted Boston: Houghton Mifflin, 1990.)

Empire, July 23, 1978.

Feitz, Leland. *Ghost Towns of the Cripple Creek District.* Colorado Springs, CO: Little London Press, 1974.

Fifer, Barbara. *Montana Mining Ghost Towns.* Helena, MT: Farcountry Press, 2002.

Granruth, Alan. *A Guide to Downtown Central City, Colorado.* Black Hawk, CO: One Stop Printing and Graphics, 1989. (Revised 1991.)

Idaho Falls Post Register, August 15, 2003 and June 16, 2007.

Idaho State Historical Series, nos. 209 (August 1976), 215 (August 1976), and 940 (June 1992). Boise, ID: Idaho State Historical Society.

Idaho State Historical Society Reference Series, no. 169. Boise ID: Idaho State Historical Society, 1980.

Levine. Brian. *Cripple Creek: City of Influence.* Cripple Creek, CO: Historic Preservation Department, City of Cripple Creek, 1994.

Lingenfelter, Richard. *Death Valley and the Amargosa: A Land of Illusion.* Berkeley and Los Angeles, CA: University of California Press, 1986.

McCollum, Oscar Jr. *Marble: A Town Built on Dreams,* volumes 1 and 2. Denver: Sundance Publications Ltd., vol. 1, 1992; vol. 2, 1993.

McCoy, Michael. *Wyoming: Off the Beaten Path.* Old Saybrook, CT: Globe Pequot Press, 1996, 1999.

Mead, Jay, ed. *Silver Plume Walking Tour.* Silver Plume, CO: People for Silver Plume, n.d.

Miller, Donald C. *Ghost Towns of Nevada.* Boulder, CO: Pruett Publishing Company, 1979.

Montana Magazine, May-June 2007.

Moynihan, Betty. *Augusta Tabor: A Pioneering Woman.* Evergreen, CO: Cordillera Press, 1988.

Murray, Robert. *Miner's Delight, Investor's Despair: The Ups and Downs of a Sub-Marginal Mining Camp in Wyoming.* Sheridan, WY: Piney Creek Press, 1972.

Neely, Cynthia, Walter R. Borneman, and Christine Bradley. *Guide to the Georgetown-Silver Plume Historic District.* Boulder, CO: Johnson Printing, 1995.

Noel, Thomas J., Paul F. Mahoney, and Richard E. Stevens. *Historical Atlas of Colorado.* Norman, OK, and London: University of Oklahoma Press, 1994.

Osterwald, Doris B. *Cinders and Smoke*. Lakewood, CO: Western Guideways, Ltd., 1965. (Sixth edition 1989.)

Packard, Howard A. Jr. *Gold Dredge on the Yankee Fork*. Great Falls, MT: Yankee Fork Publishing, 1983.

Paher, Stanley W. *Nevada Ghost Towns and Mining Camps*. Berkeley, CA: Howell-North Books, 1970.

———. *Nevada Ghost Towns and Mining Camps Atlas*. Las Vegas: Nevada Publications, 2006.

Patera, Alan H. *Belmont, Nevada*. Lake Grove, OR: Western Places, 2005.

Powell, Allan Kent. *The Next Time We Strike: Labor in Utah's Coal Fields*. Logan, UT: Utah State University Press, 1985.

Sparling, Wayne. *Southern Idaho Ghost Towns*. Caldwell, ID: The Caxton Printers, Ltd., 1976.

Stoehr, C. Eric. *Bonanza Victorian*. Albuquerque, NM: University of New Mexico Press, 1975.

Twain, Mark. *Roughing It*. New York: Penguin Books, 1981. (Originally published by American Publishing Company, 1872.)

Ubbelohde, Carl, Maxine Benson, and Duane A. Smith. *A Colorado History*, 7th ed. Boulder, CO: Pruett Publishing Company, 1995.

Varney, Philip. *Ghost Towns of Colorado*. Stillwater, MN: Voyageur Press, 1999.

———. *Southern California's Best Ghost Towns*. Norman, OK, and London: University of Oklahoma Press, 1990.

Wall Street Journal, October 11, 2005.

Weight, Harold and Lucille. *Rhyolite: The Ghost City of Golden Dreams*. Twentynine Palms, CA: The Calico Press, 1978.

Wolle, Muriel Sibell. *The Bonanza Trail*. Chicago: Swallow Press, 1953.

———. *Stampede to Timberline*. Chicago: Swallow Press, 1949. (Revised 1974.)

Zauner, Phyllis and Lou Zauner. *Virginia City: A Mini-History*. Tahoe Paradise, CA: Zanel Publications, 1979.

BIBLIOGRAPHY

INDEX

ABOUT THE AUTHOR AND PHOTOGRAPHER

PHILIP VARNEY is the author of seven ghost town guidebooks, including *Ghost Towns of the Pacific Northwest, Ghost Towns of Northern California, Arizona's Ghost Towns and Mining Camps,* and *Ghost Towns of Colorado.*

Varney visited his first ghost town—Central City, Colorado—at the age of eleven and has been an enthusiast ever since. A former high school English teacher and department chairman, he has toured and photographed more than six hundred ghost towns throughout the American West.

In addition to his ghost town books, Varney has authored a book on bicycle tours of southern Arizona, was a contributing writer for Insight Guide's *Wild West,* and has been a contributor to *Arizona Highways* magazine.

Philip Varney lives in Tucson, Arizona.